MAD rhapsody

MAD rhapsody

Ma Yansong

Philip Jodidio

foreword by Paul Goldberger

MAD rhapsody

RIZZOLI Electa

contents

allegory

chromatic harmony

Architecture is a discipline that has both internal and external constraints. Within the field, architecture has long been discussed in terms of particular styles, languages, forms, materials, or ways of thinking. Externally, it is restricted by commercial, branding, and political factors. These all become self-restrictions that prevent architecture from initiating a deeper dialogue with the world.

How might we respond to this complicated world and really dive into its richness? I don't think it is a chaotic process, or a uniform one. Perhaps it could be more focused on the uniqueness of every project, responding to the particular cultural and social traits of the sites. Every architectural project should have its own destination.

The work of MAD is like a rhapsody. The name MAD itself means madness, representing a rebellious and critical attitude. It also manifests an opposition to a generic pattern, goal, form, or language. I am intrigued by responding to the real world with diverse, genuine, and live emotions.

Architecture should not be treated as a result but as a reflection: a reflection on the atmosphere of the site, time, and human spirit, as well as emotions. These factors naturally give architecture subjectivity and uniqueness. It is the architect's ego, but it is more than the ego. It is like an independent verse of a rhapsody that evokes emotions deep inside. Such an episode is inspired by real life with spontaneous sensations and therefore has a folkloric character.

When I saw goldfish being sold on the street, I thought about people who struggled to make a living in the city. My compassion drove me to design a fish tank that represents a more dignified way of living.

When a Japanese father and son hesitated about tearing down their old house in order to build a homelike kindergarten, I suggested that the wooden skeleton of the old house could be preserved. Ultimately it was seen as a continuation of both the memories and the lives once lived here, creating an emotional connection between the past and the present.

When I saw the old city of Beijing was gradually being dominated by generic high-rises, I built a solitary black peak as an homage to the spirit of classical landscape. It also opposes the modern values of "higher, faster, and stronger," standing in the midst of other skyscrapers like a lone knight.

When I see all kinds of fake antiques that are built in the name of "preserving the appearance of the ancient city," a reflective shining bubble pops up in my mind. The result does not have any particular historic attributes, but actively fights for the authenticity and independence of history.

When I was in a cave in Japan enjoying the landscape and being bathed in natural light, I felt the semicircular scenery framed by the cave should be turned into a whole circle. I achieved that with a reflective metal surface and water landscape within the cave. Visitors can walk into the circle and mediate between the earth and the sky.

When the father of *Star Wars* decided to build a museum for younger generations, I couldn't suppress my curiosity about his universe. Curiosity comes from the awe of the unknown.

When I saw exhausted people walking through the "grand" palaces and monuments in the city, I designed a place of spiritual freedom, where the buildings would disappear into the landscape, so people could slow down and look into the deepest parts of their hearts.

My reactions to and emotions about different things drag me into completely different worlds. *MAD Rhapsody* is emotional, immersive, and full of variations, rhythms, and moods. The juxtaposition of various feelings creates a dislocation and reorganization of time and space. I do not think time is linear, and I do not have any particular preference for the past or the future. By juxtaposing multiple times and spaces, I can enter a broader temporality.

This rhapsody may not have a fixed formal structure, appearance, or uniform pattern of development and organization. It is spontaneous, improvised, and free. It celebrates individual emotions. It is a folk epic that makes fantasy a reality.

What to make of an architect who says, "My curves are different. I try to make them somehow strange," who talks of Louis Kahn but whose work makes you think that he is the love child of Antoni Gaudí and Archigram? I don't like to talk about architects in terms of other architects, but with Ma Yansong you have to start there, because his architecture seems, when you first encounter it, to tease you with its echoes of the work of others. It is hard, for example, not to look at Ma's strong, curving shapes and think not only of Gaudí but also of Zaha Hadid, for whom Ma worked early in his career. Or of Frederick Kiesler and his "endless house," or of some of the more extravagant midcentury creations of Eero Saarinen or Wallace K. Harrison: buildings that do not seem confined by the rational insistence on orthogonal form, that seem antithetical to the grid, that seem to want to stand alone.

And then you get through all of that and you realize that Ma Yansong and his firm, MAD Architects, are not like any of these other architects at all. Ma has assimilated all of these influences, tempered them with a sensitivity to both Chinese and Western urbanism and the Chinese vernacular, added a dollop of pure fantasy and perhaps a bit of science fiction, and come up with a series of architectural statements that, if nothing else, seem entirely of the twenty-first century: technologically adventuresome, flamboyant, bold and monumental in scale, yet with surprising and endearing elements of intimacy. This is architecture that has the romantic appeal of old-style futurism, filtered through the blob architecture sensibility of the digital age, and produced by a sophisticated maker of form who knows how developers think and is able to convince them to come along with him and do it his way. MAD's groupings of skyscrapers, projects like the Nanjing Zendai Himalayas Center with its thirteen white towers, and the Chaoyang Park Plaza in Beijing with its multiple black towers, are unlike any multibuilding urban developments I have ever seen. They are not new interpretations of Rockefeller Center, or echoes of any Western complex of towers at all; they are something entirely, dramatically, different—sets of towers that look more like mountains, buildings intended to evoke a natural landscape, not to sit discreetly before one.

Are Ma Yansong's shapes truly nature, or is the suggestion that they are a romantic indulgence? I would say more the latter, but what of it? This is not a rationalist architecture and it is not a functionalist architecture and it is not a minimalist architecture; it is an architecture of image, of feeling, and of emotion, which puts it, for all its daring, in a line of descent from so much architecture, both Western and Asian, that seeks to evoke visual effect in quest of emotional impact. Nanjing

has an almost cartoonlike quality, and I do not mean that as a negative comment. It is how Ma Yansong humanizes the vast scale he is dealing with here. He does not truly want to fool us into thinking his buildings are mountains; rather, he has made his buildings a kind of playful, cartoon version of mountains, which makes the large-scale urbanism he is trying to devise seem accessible. Some architects play in the fields of the architecture of the past in search of emotional connection; Ma Yansong plays in the fields of nature, expropriating it for visual pleasure.

This is altogether different from those architects who claim nature as an inspiration for structural systems, such as Buckminster Fuller, whose work, for all its utopianism, has none of MAD's romantic, playful quality and is driven by a search for rational structure more than visual pleasure. The most revealing thing I have ever heard Ma Yansong say about his work is that it is the shape that matters to him, not the structure; that while of course he thinks about structure and materials as every architect must, forms and shapes are where his passions lie. He designs them intuitively, which means that the resemblance to, say, Hadid is at best a superficial one. This is not an architecture driven by parametric theory or, indeed, by any theory at all other than a kind of exuberant embrace of visual drama, contorted into urban form.

Ma Yansong's aesthetic is sculptural, but that doesn't mean that his architecture is sculpture. It means that he designs buildings whose forms are striking, whose shapes are memorable and visually powerful and almost never resemble the shapes of the buildings around them. The instinct that led Frank Lloyd Wright to put the Guggenheim Museum's curves amid the boxy apartment buildings of Fifth Avenue lives within Ma Yansong all the time; when he received a commission to do an apartment tower in New York called EAST 34th, he proposed a gently tapering form that looked like a vast Brancusi. His proposed Tower in downtown Toronto is a forty-eight-story-high, sinuous arc, a tower at once vertical and horizontal, a croquet wicket in glass.

Such huge complexes as the Nanjing and Beijing projects, not to mention Sanya Phoenix Island in Sanya in southern China, the Absolute Towers in Mississauga, Ontario, Canada (the project that first gained MAD international attention), and Fake Hills in Beihai, China—a striking mega-building in the form of an enormous undulating wall—suggest that MAD's work is primarily focused on ways in which visual pleasure and surprise can mitigate the vastness of contemporary urban scale. But just as often, Ma's fascination with shape leads to single buildings of conventional size that are, for all intents and purposes, self-referential pieces

of swirling architectural form, their curving surfaces wrapped around program. The Harbin Opera House in Harbin, China, and the Ordos Museum in Ordos, China, are perhaps the best known of these, but before long the Lucas Museum of Narrative Art, now under construction in Los Angeles (following earlier designs by Ma for sites in Chicago and San Francisco), will probably eclipse them both as Ma's first major institutional project in the United States. The Lucas design owes no small debt to the earlier Harbin project, which Sir Peter Cook wrote is a building that "causes us to sit up and salivate . . . for me, its exhilaration is simply the product of a far more inventive and fearless motivation than being merely responsive or quotational."

Fair enough, although Ma has the ability, when he chooses, to be responsive or quotational, at least on his own terms. There is the Conrad Hotel in Beijing, which softly plays at being a conventional tower, its inflections and curves more subtle than MAD's usual; or MAD's first building to be completed in Los Angeles, the 8600 Wilshire Boulevard condominium complex Gardenhouse, which gently evokes the classic Los Angeles image of modern houses atop a landscaped hillside in the form of an array of little gable-roofed structures poking out of a "living wall"—a building that at once celebrates context and wittily turns it into something else.

There is a certain playfulness to Gardenhouse, and even more so to another of my favorite of MAD's smaller projects, the lovely and gracious Courtyard Kindergarten in Beijing, where a traditional Chinese courtyard building is surrounded by a version of one of MAD's swirling forms, this time with a red roof used for play; the entire complex is a dialogue between new and old, open and enclosed, freedom and order that is at once a whimsical exercise and a serious lesson in historical juxtaposition. Here, the interplay between Ma Yansong's own curving shapes and the orthogonal world that existed before them happens within the bounds of the project itself. But for all that the dialectic between the historic core and MAD's sensual curves defines the Courtyard Kindergarten, Ma's shapes can often make a convincing world of their own, as at the immense Quzhou Sports Campus in Quzhou, China, a complex of stadiums and training facilities in which the swooping curves of MAD's buildings slide in and out and over and under manmade, landscaped hills to yield what MAD calls "the world's largest earth-sheltered architecture"—an earthwork as much as a series of buildings.

Quzhou Sports Campus will function as a park as well as an athletic complex, and it underscores the extent to which many of the MAD projects seek to serve as public space as well as private environments. That is certainly true of both Yiwu Grand Theater, now rising in Yiwu, China, and Shenzhen Bay Culture Park, under construction in Shenzhen, China. Both are waterfront projects, and both seek to open their cities' waterfronts to public use, although there the similarity ends, since they show opposite sides of Ma Yansong's shape-making inclinations. Shenzhen Bay Culture Park will contain the Creative Design Hall and the Shenzhen Science and Technology Museum, whose various wings are housed in very MAD-esque, curving shapes that will sit, like a carefully arranged set of smooth boulders, within and under a landscaped park. It is assertively sculptural, and the rounded forms, though light in color, read as heavy, solid masses. Yiwu Grand Theater, by contrast, seems a bit more like a conventional building—not too conventional, of course, since this is, after all, the work of MAD. But with its layers of curving glass canopies set around a boxy central structure, it evokes Frank Gehry's Fondation Louis Vuitton, as its interior loosely calls to mind Gehry's Walt Disney Concert Hall. The overall effect of Yiwu's glowing, curving panels of glass, sitting on the waterfront, is a lightness that makes it very different from the Shenzhen project. In the end, it provides a subtler kind of drama in the way it gently but emphatically tilts toward what might be called the architecturally normative—not too much, of course, but just enough to create a pleasing tension between Ma Yansong's world of shapes and the world of buildings that we know.

Both the UNIC residential tower in Paris and the 71 Via Boncompagni residential complex in Rome also have that same quality of existing in a kind of sweet spot between fanciful shape-making and architectural familiarity, and both bring an easy, relaxed quality to traditional cityscapes—in Paris through Ma's characteristic undulating form and in Rome through an elegant, modernist composition that seems to float on the streetscape. In both cities, Ma Yansong's buildings dance on the edge of convention, determinedly different from what is around them and yet in a wonderful way the same. They fit in the same way that Gaudí's apartment buildings fit in Barcelona: as exclamation points in the urban landscape. That is what Ma Yansong does everywhere, at every scale: he uses architecture to bring moments of easy, relaxed joy.

The word rhapsody implies a high degree of emotion or even a state of rapture. In music it is defined as a "composition of irregular form having an improvisatory character." The German writer Johann Wolfgang von Goethe (1749–1832) famously said, "I have found a sheet among my papers . . . where I call architecture frozen music. And really . . . the mood that emanates from architecture comes close to the effect of music."[1] Nor is this relation without consequence in the reasoning of Goethe, who viewed musical tones as "monads," which is to say elementary individual substances that reflect the order of the world. Before Goethe, the Italian philosopher and mathematician Giordano Bruno (1548–1600) identified three fundamental types of monads: God, souls, and atoms.[2] By this reasoning, harkening back to the essential nature of the tone, architecture, too, can (should?) reflect the order of the world and of life—not an idea that has been prevalent in most contemporary architecture.

Goethe could not have imagined the future evolution of music, yet the analogy he established is still relevant. Frozen music still, but the music and architecture of our time, and ultimately tones and works that reflect primary concepts. Which music might best correspond to the unexpected oeuvre of Ma Yansong, who founded MAD Architects in 2004? Are the Ordos Museum and the Absolute Towers in Canada more than solo performances by a virtuoso, or are they part of a broader composition, one that might be called a rhapsody? Not a Hungarian Rhapsody by Franz Liszt or even George Gershwin's 1924 *Rhapsody in Blue*, but instead something closer to our time, something even more emotional, effusive, or possibly extravagant?

"Bohemian Rhapsody" is an unusual six-minute song by the British group Queen. Written by Freddie Mercury, it was part of the 1975 album *A Night at the Opera*. Disconcerting, even unprecedented, "Bohemian Rhapsody" is made up of six sections, each in a different musical style: an intro, a ballad, a guitar solo, opera followed by hard rock, and, finally, a more reflective outro. The song became hugely popular, even as critics seemed to have doubts precisely because it was difficult to classify the work. In 2009, *The Guardian* explained:

> The precedents of "Bohemian Rhapsody" are as much in the nineteenth-century classical traditions of rhapsodic, quasi-improvisational reveries—like, say, the piano works of Schumann or Chopin or the tone-poems of Strauss or Liszt—as they are in prog-rock or the contemporary pop of 1975. That's because the song manages a sleight of musical hand that only a handful of real master-musicians have managed: the illusion that its huge variety of styles—from intro, to ballad,

to operatic excess, to hard-rock, to reflective coda—are unified into a single statement, a drama that somehow makes sense. It's a classic example of the unity in diversity that high-minded musical commentators have heard in the symphonies of Beethoven or the operas of Mozart. And that's exactly what the piece is: a miniature operatic-rhapsodic-symphonic-tone-poem.[3]

It is not a coincidence that this book is called *MAD Rhapsody*. Freddie Mercury's 1975 classic is a favorite of Ma Yansong. Although the architect sets aside more specific parallels, the combination of different moods and styles in "Bohemian Rhapsody" may offer a way to better understand the work of MAD. Then, too, a "composition of irregular form having an improvisatory character" could well describe types of music and architecture, but it also could be a deeper evocation of the order of the world, and of life itself. Like "Bohemian Rhapsody," the work of MAD does not appear as a neatly ordered system or style; instead it is a flowing combination of forces and forms that has more to do with Surrealism and science fiction and an unrestrained imagination than it does with the strict Euclidean vision of modernism.

Allegorical Bridges

MAD, founded in 2004 by Ma Yansong, first gained attention in 2006 when the firm won an international competition to design the first project in this book, the Absolute Towers near Toronto, completed in 2012. These surprising, undulating towers are respectively 170 meters (557 feet) and 150 meters (492 feet) high. According to the architect, "The Absolute Towers parallel the twisting fluidity or natural lines found in life." Completed one year before the Absolute Towers, the Ordos Museum (Inner Mongolia, China, 2011), in which the artist Ai Weiwei and the architects Herzog & de Meuron were also involved, was intended as a centerpiece for a new city. With a design influenced both by the work of Buckminster Fuller and by the neighboring Gobi Desert, the Ordos Museum marked another surprising, powerful element in the emerging forms created by MAD. As the architect puts it, "Familiar yet distinct, the museum in Ordos appears to have either landed in the desert from another world or to always have existed." The idea of creating links between the ancient past still present in China with futuristic forms is a recurring theme in MAD's work. Another of the firm's projects, the Pingtan Art Museum, is set on an artificial island that is reached by crossing an allegorical bridge between "artificial and natural, city and culture, history and future," according to the firm's own description. The Absolute Towers and the Ordos Museum are among the most frequently published works of contemporary architecture in recent years. They are the visible sign of the rise of MAD Architects and its form-driven sense of drama. They draw attention, they look like few buildings ever built before, and, still, they serve their purpose well.

The Shenzhen Bay Culture Park has a built area of no less than 182,000 square meters (1,959,000 square feet) on a site with an outdoor amphitheater that can seat 10,000 people. "I want to create a surreal atmosphere, so that the people who visit, relax, or exercise here have the possibility to engage in a dialogue with the past and the future. Time and space are dissolved and placed over each other, manifesting a sense of unrestrained imagination," says Ma Yansong.

Hard rock emerged in the late 1960s and early 1970s with groups such as Led Zeppelin, AC/DC, Deep Purple, and Queen. With strong, even aggressive vocals, soaring electric guitars, and pounding drums, hard rock might appear to be in contradiction to opera, or might it be a more effusive version of storytelling? According to Ma Yansong, the forms of the Lucas Museum of Narrative Art were inspired by the canopy of trees. The fluidity of the design has a direct bearing on the rhythm of narrative or the storytelling that is a fundamental aspect of the work of George Lucas. If the Lucas Museum brings to mind any frozen music, it is definitely rock 'n' roll.

Chromatic Harmony
An opera is a drama set to music and made up of vocal pieces with orchestral accompaniment and orchestral overtures and interlude. The designs of MAD Architects have evolved toward more complex and significant works, such as the Harbin Opera House, which takes on the forms of the wetlands from which it rises. The scale and ambition of the project are laid out in the firm's own description: "The Harbin Opera House was envisioned as the cultural center of the future—a tremendous performance venue, as well as a dramatic public space that embodies the integration of humanity, art, and local identity. It is an iconic landmark for the city of Harbin and an important public space for its citizens, and it encourages exploration of and participation in the city's cultural endeavors." An operatic scale indeed, and a sense of composition that reaches into sources of inspiration that are intimately related, even as they seem to have been registered in different keys, forming a kind of chromatic harmony.

Elemental Landscapes
The Tunnel of Light is another of MAD's projects that has been broadly published, offering as it does astonishing views from a disused 750-meter (2,460-foot) tunnel in the mountains of Japan. Five installations based on water, fire, earth, metal, and wood are brought together in an orchestration that owes nothing to the architectural forms of the past, but that does amplify the experience of visitors in new ways. As the architect puts it, "Tunnel of Light allows visitors to transcend the role of observer and to become active participants. It allows individuals to place themselves in nature in unexpected ways."

According to the architect, the Yiwu Grand Theater is "positioned with the mountains in the distance as its backdrop, and the water as its stage," allowing it to appear to float on the river. The theater is separated from a nearby conference center by a densely planted valley. As a result of this and other elements of the design, the "theater offers an immersive natural experience that feels far from its urban setting." The emphasis on nature demonstrated here is indicative of a broader approach to large contemporary buildings. Where urban context was considered important in some contemporary architecture, MAD seeks in a way to create a new natural context that is in keeping with the cities concerned while it creates spaces that are made up of not only concrete, glass, and steel.

Spark of Life
The conclusion of "Bohemian Rhapsody," the outro, reverts to a calmer, more reflective mode. On a much smaller scale than some of MAD's best-known projects, the Hutong Bubble project directly addresses the question of the modernization of historic urban residential areas. Specifically concerned in this instance are alleyways in Beijing, which are typically lined with traditional courtyard houses. Rather than demolishing old buildings, the architects instead added a series of smooth, mirrored metal bubbles, connecting spaces and adding places for contemplation to rooftops while participating in the renovation of the existing houses. Undeniably modern and organic in form, the bubbles "allow old and new to complement one another." Further, Ma Yansong says, "This is a micro-utopian ideal. I hope that these bubbles will serve as vital newborn cells, giving the traditional *hutong* new life and revitalizing the community." In these cases and others in the repertory of MAD, there is an organic component that somehow seems not to contradict futuristic forms. With contemplation and calm comes an effortless bridging of supposed opposites.

The Jiaxing Train Station is a large (354,000-square-meter/3,810,424-square-foot) facility that is unusual because it is mostly underground, leaving space above for a forest park. The concern demonstrated by the architects for the natural environment and the city brings a new idea of life into the heart of a city of 1.3 million inhabitants.

The FENIX Museum of Migration being built in a former warehouse in the port of Rotterdam is the first public cultural building in Europe to be designed by a Chinese architect. At its center, a vortex-shaped stairway spirals up through the structure and above its roof to provide views of the port. Like a tornado, or a spark of life rising from the past, the stairway is clearly symbolic of the wealth of opportunities brought by migrants to this place.

Music of the Future
The idea of the rhapsody, especially the multipart composition of apparent opposites imagined by Freddie Mercury, does fit well with the projects of MAD. In the firm's work, there is a willful integration or combination of forces that seem contradictory into a coherent whole. It finds forms that are at once astonishing and still not fundamentally out of place. Past and present, artificial and natural, rigid and supple are brought together into what must be described as a fluid vocabulary. Zaha Hadid found inspiration in the angled works of the Russian Constructivists, also imagining buildings as landscape in a rigorous challenge of architecture as it was. Ma Yansong has surely been less doctrinaire and freer, as the swirling image of "Bohemian Rhapsody" might imply. There is more than form in his message; there is also an intoxicating sense that architecture can still reinvent the world, that it can connect what was and what will be. Frozen music, yes, but the music of the future, a release of the fundamental forces and influences whose relative absence has so constrained modern architecture.

Freddie Mercury said, "It's one of those songs which has such a fantasy feel about it. I think people should just listen to it, think about it, and then make up their own minds as to what it says to them . . . 'Bohemian Rhapsody' didn't just come out of thin air." The word rhapsody, which is, once again, a "composition of irregular form having an improvisatory character," explains the juxtaposition of a ballad, a solo sequence, hard rock, opera, and a conclusion, or outro. These changing moods are brought together by the voice of Freddie Mercury and the musicians of Queen, and so, too, with no undue exaggeration are the flowing, surging, operatic, living forms imagined by Ma Yansong and MAD. The reason that "Bohemian Rhapsody" still resonates for people almost fifty years after it was written is that there is an underlying familiarity in the palette of musical elements that weaves the composition together. There is an energy, an authenticity, and a voice that bring it all into focus, a force of life expressed. Lost for so many years

in formal compositions that often were more rooted in geometry and economics than they were in life, contemporary architecture seems to have been waiting for an eruption of imagination that links past, present, and future, nature and artifice, emotion and programmatic requirements. This is not a new style, but instead a liberation of fundamental forces, with each sequence (or work of architecture) intimately linked to time and reality, to harmony and landscape, and, finally, to life. *MAD Rhapsody* is a search for the rhapsody of life in built form.

Notes
1. Johann Peter Eckermann, "Conversations with Goethe/Part II, 23.3.1829," accessed December 15, 2020, https://lueersen.homedns.org/!gutenb/eckerman /gesprche/gsp2026.htm: "'Ich habe unter meinen Papieren ein Blatt gefunden,' sagte Goethe heute, 'wo ich die Baukunst eine erstarrte Musik nenne. Und wirklich, es hat etwas; die Stimmung, die von der Baukunst ausgeht, kommt dem Effekt der Musik nahe.'"
2. "Giordano Bruno" in *Stanford Encyclopedia of Philosophy*: https://plato.stanford.edu /entries/bruno/. The close relationship of the thoughts of Goethe to those of Giordano Bruno has been asserted by, among others, Rudolf Steiner in "Galileo, Giordano Bruno, and Goethe," a lecture given in Berlin on January 26, 1911: https://wn.rsarchive.org /Lectures/19110126p01.html.
3. Tom Service, "Bohemian Rhapsody: Mamma, We've Killed a Song," *The Guardian*, December 7, 2009. https://www.theguardian.com/music/2009/dec/08 /bohemian-rhapsody-karaoke-hit

allegory

The Absolute Towers are a twin residential high-rise buildings located in Mississauga, Ontario, Canada. The form of the buildings parallels the twisting fluidity of lines found in nature. The torsional form rises from an organic punctuation in concrete—a boxed landscape, making Absolute Towers not only a cultural symbol of Mississauga but also a new paradigm for high-rises in generic North American cities.

Bordered by Toronto on the east, Mississauga has quickly developed into an independent urbanized area. It faced the challenge of establishing a unique character and responding to growing needs from residents. Sited at the junction of two main streets, the twin towers welcome traffic from the south headed north as a gateway to the city beyond. MAD saw the opportunity for the city to expand in a more approachable and organic way.

absolute towers

The design breaks away from functionalist principles. It embodies resistance to modernism and Le Corbusier's famous motto "a house is a machine for living in." Throughout the process of urbanization, skyscrapers have become homogeneous, linear structures in a process of degenerative duplication across the globe. The Absolute Towers imagine an urban forest, contrary to horizontals and verticals, embracing sensual curves and open individual spaces connected with consistency that rebuild urban life with nuance and lively activities.

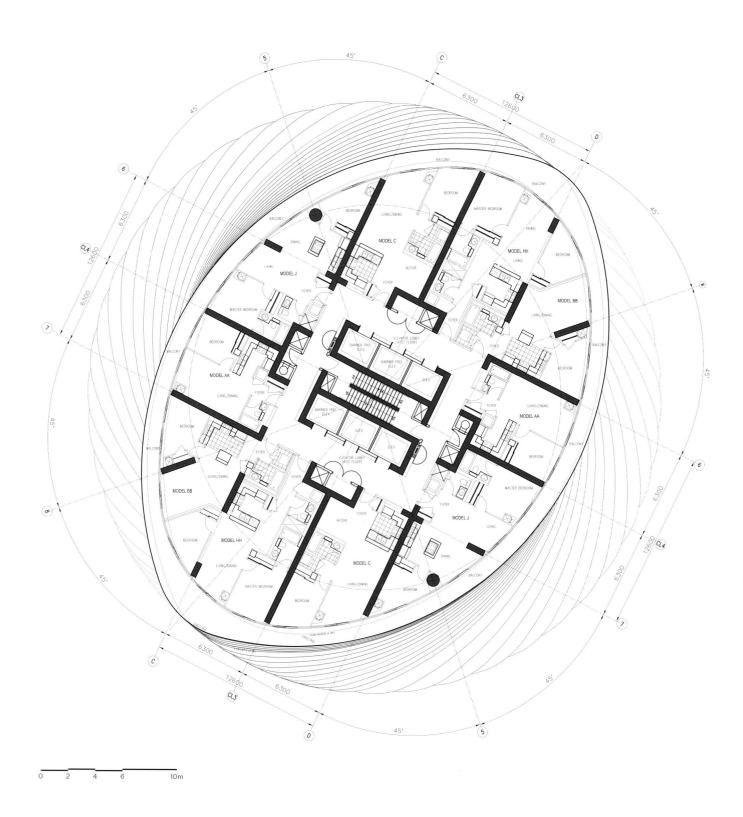

absolute towers

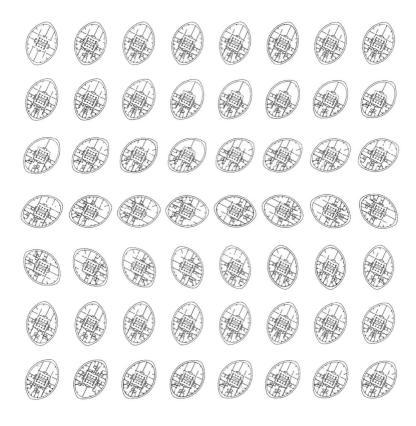

The Absolute Towers consist of two high-rise buildings. Continuous and extended balconies become the new frontier of the facade, wrapping the architecture with an active, eventful, and breathable exterior space. Each floor has a consistent oval shape and rotates from one to eight degrees, providing each resident with a unique panorama of the city. It promotes community at the microscale of a single floor by eliminating vertical barriers traditionally used in high-rise architecture. At the macro scale, the cadence of the floors rising into the sky echoes human experience, evoking the movement of an adoring figure.

The torsional form of the towers is supported by a surprisingly simple yet efficient structure. A grid of concrete load-bearing walls extends and contracts in response to the sectional fluctuation created by the rotation of the floors. The naturally aerodynamic and fluid shaping of the towers adeptly handles wind loads and ensures comfort throughout the balconies.

After the completion of Absolute Towers in 2012, a deep emotional bond was generated between local residents and the architecture. They became the backdrop for many people's lives on social media, and this landmark was fondly dubbed "Marilyn Monroe," as it was seen as sharing the famed actress's sensibility and enthusiasm.

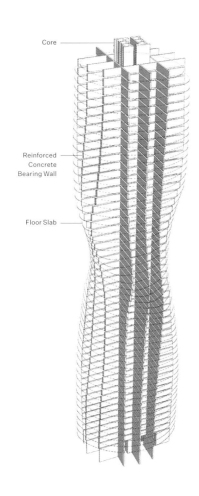

the cloudscape of haikou   2021 / Haikou, China

The Cloudscape of Haikou is located in Century Park along the Haikou Bay coastline. It is a multi-functional building that can host people for reading and at the same time provides a public rest area for visitors.

Sited in a key area of the Hainan free-trade island initiative, the project is part of a government-launched enterprise to rejuvenate Haikou Bay. With great views of the seascape and balmy weather, the open area along the coastline was awaiting a critical anchor that would fully transform it into a welcoming public space for rest and relaxation. The Cloudscape of Haikou is the first completed project in the area master plan.

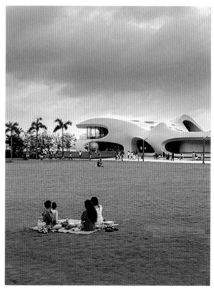

the cloudscape of haikou

The interior and exterior of the building are cast in fair-faced concrete to create a single cohesive, flowing form. It is composed of a 690-square-meter (7,425-square-foot) reading space with café and terrace, and a 300-square-meter (3,230-square-foot) public relaxation area that is equipped with a bicycle parking system, public restrooms, and shower areas. Throughout the building, burrows offer individual retreat spaces. Different "caves" house diversified programs; on the second floor, the concrete shape opens up to reveal a tunnel that leads people from an exterior platform to the interior. Varied openings allow sunlight to flood the rooms. Inside the library, people confront the sky and sea directly. Humans are no longer the key players, and architecture is no longer the prime mover. Instead, people's integrated experiences offer a glimpse of the universe—abstract and infinite.

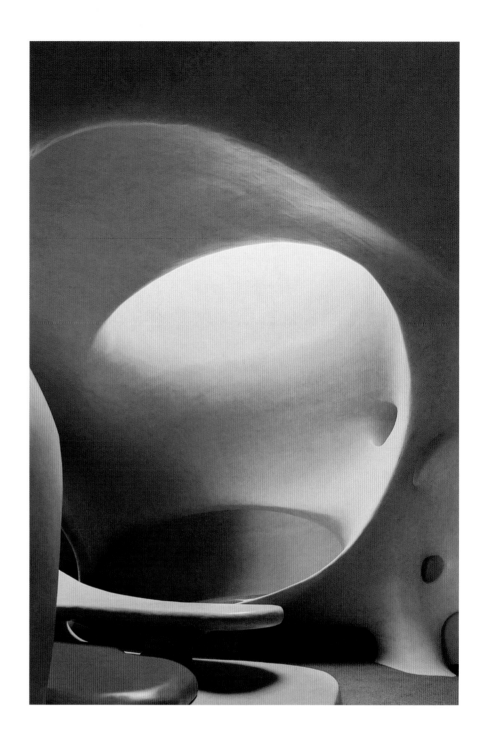

To ensure accuracy and seamlessness across the undulating surfaces, the building units were cast using both CNC [computer numerical control] and a 3D-printed model. The MEP [mechanical, electrical, and plumbing] system is designed to be hidden within concrete cavities to minimize its visibility and to underline visual consistency. The roof, on the sunny side, is cantilevered to guarantee comfortable temperatures, realizing a sustainable and energy-saving building that responds to local weather. Curved sliding doors and retractable glass curtain walls make breathable openings that enhance the overall airflow and ventilation.

The pavilion gets its name from its resemblance to clouds floating softly through the sky. The skillful articulation of the passages echoes the idea of integrated landscape and an open atmosphere that encourages the development of artistic life. As Haikou's latest energetic popular public space, it will bring layers of color to the city.

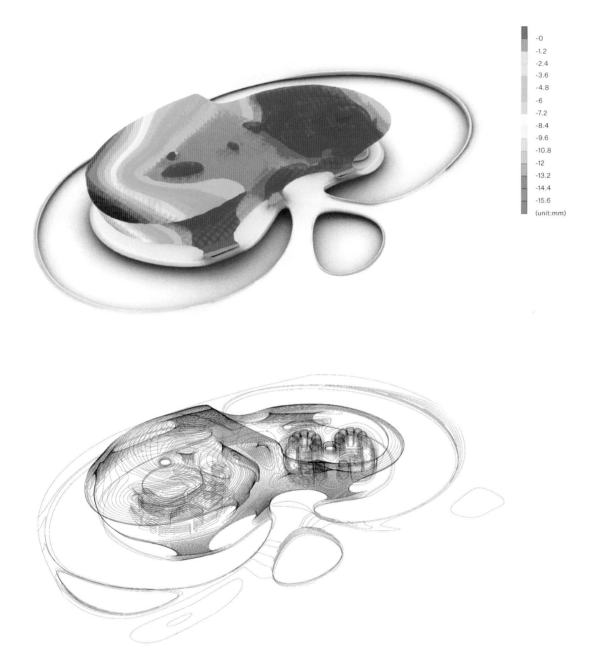

-0
-1.2
-2.4
-3.6
-4.8
-6
-7.2
-8.4
-9.6
-10.8
-12
-13.2
-14.4
-15.6
(unit:mm)

the cloudscape of haikou

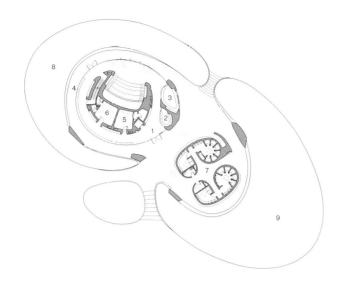

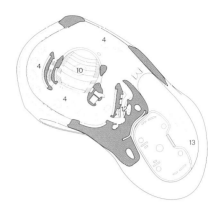

N   0   5   10   15m

1. Main Entrance	8. White Sand
2. Reception	9. Reflecting Pool
3. Café	10. Auditorium
4. Reading Space	11. Kids' Playroom
5. Office	12. Terrace
6. Multifunction/VIP Room	
7. Bathroom	

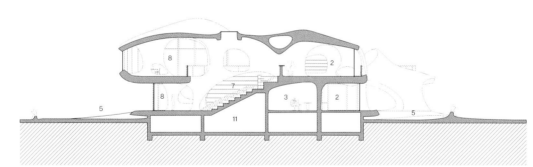

1. Café
2. Reading Space
3. Multifunction/VIP Room
4. Bathroom
5. Sand Pool
6. Reflecting Pool
7. Stepped Reading Space
8. Ocean View Reading Space
9. Kids' Reading Space
10. Roof Garden
11. MEP

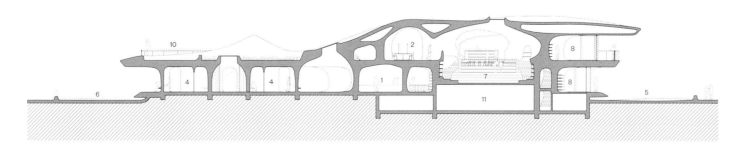

0   5   10   15m

Situated between the vibrant urban energy of Shenzhen and the natural tranquility of the ocean, Shenzhen Bay Culture Park is a complex that manifests as a piece of "land art." The park's artistic, delicate urban landscape evokes a timeless aura, embracing layered temporalities of both the distant past and the future.

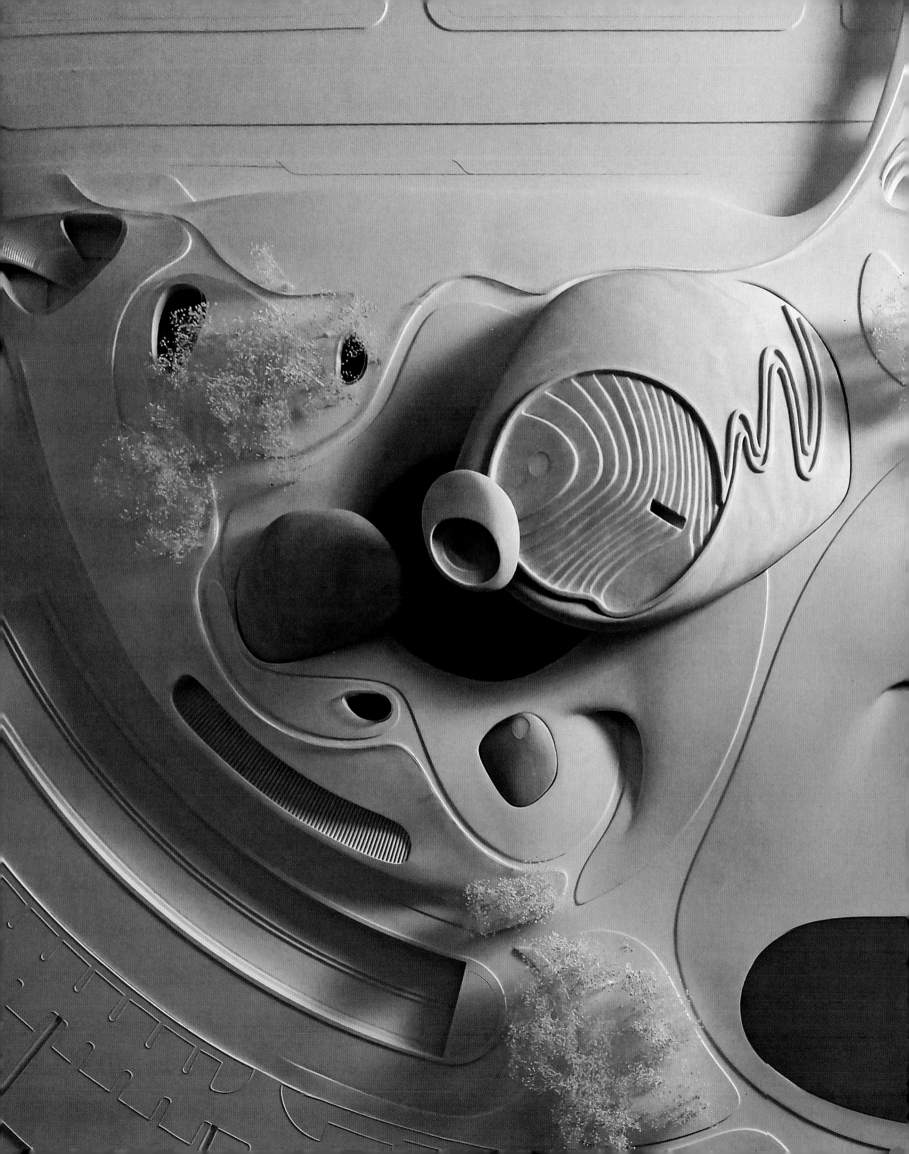

shenzhen bay culture park

The park is located in the Houhai area of Shenzhen's Nanshan district, in close proximity to the numerous corporate headquarters of the city's Central Business District. The project is one of the "ten new cultural facilities" earmarked in Shenzhen's urban development, demonstrating the city's ambition to become a creative capital on the world stage. Set against the backdrop of soaring skyscrapers, the Culture Park is envisioned as a space of freedom for citizens, serving primarily as a piece of land art, but also fulfilling its functional exhibition requirements.

Shenzhen Bay Culture Park covers an area of 51,000 square meters (549,000 square feet), with a total built area of 182,000 square meters (1,959,000 square feet), including the Creative Design Hall and the Shenzhen Science and Technology Museum. The project is formed by a sprawling green plaza and water pond, concealing a reception area, standard exhibition halls, public education space, library, auditorium, theater, café, and supporting businesses. At every turn, programmatic functions blend into the landscape. Roofs naturally slope into the ground. The sunken gardens of continuous heights and staggered amorphous masses all gravitate to the pond as a focal point: a mediator between the architecture and the landscape.

Monolithic architectural masses intersect with the undulating landscapes to form varied hardscaped spaces. The distance and relationship between each realm are carefully curated to create diversified spaces for exterior activities, mysterious entrances, or a garden of solitude. While varying in aura, these hardscaped spaces are unified by a material language that remains consistent between the interior and exterior.

shenzhen bay culture park

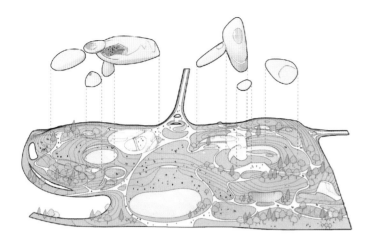

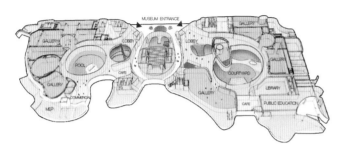

As visitors move from outside to inside, the rough stone adopts a smoothing quality, while the gaps between the massing of the building forms allow natural light to flood the interior. Within the special exhibition hall, the energy moves from land to sky, with a soaring volume reaching 30 meters (98 feet) in height. This unique gallery space accommodates a diverse display of large-scale installations, videos, multimedia, and performances, all enhanced by a backdrop of stunning architectural spatial effects. Here, visitors enter a surreal and mysterious realm, drastically different from the central business area beyond.

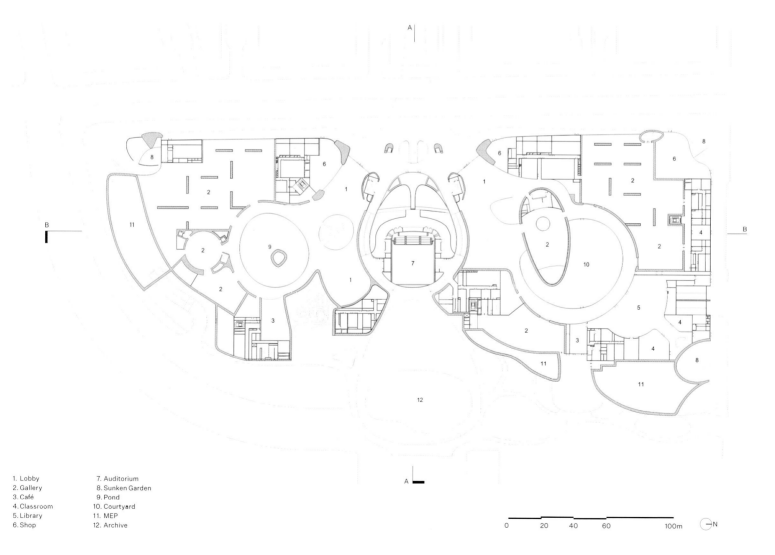

1. Lobby
2. Gallery
3. Café
4. Classroom
5. Library
6. Shop
7. Auditorium
8. Sunken Garden
9. Pond
10. Courtyard
11. MEP
12. Archive

0   20   40   60   100m   N

shenzhen bay culture park

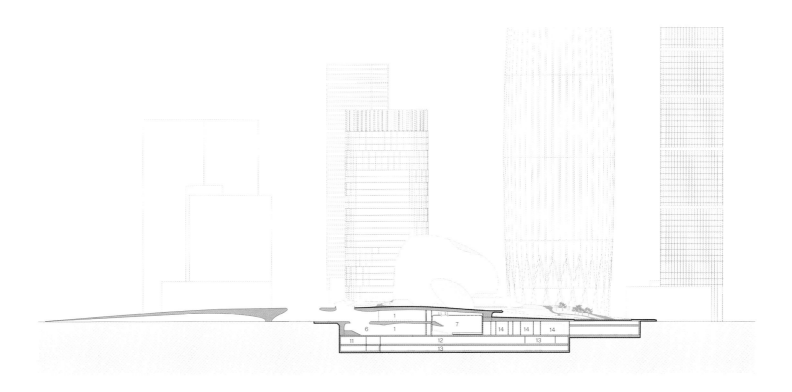

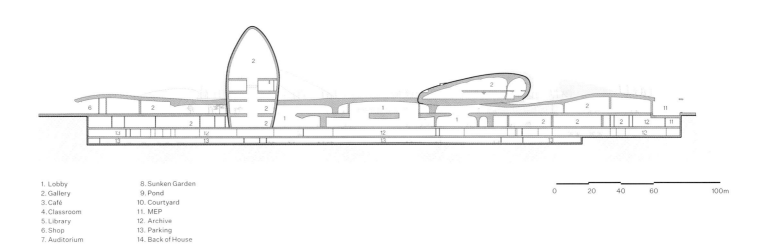

1. Lobby
2. Gallery
3. Café
4. Classroom
5. Library
6. Shop
7. Auditorium
8. Sunken Garden
9. Pond
10. Courtyard
11. MEP
12. Archive
13. Parking
14. Back of House

0   20   40   60   100m

In a connected urban context, the park is crossed by numerous pedestrian walkways and cycling paths weaving between the buildings, connecting the greater urban area with the expansive recreational space along the waterfront. Public life therefore takes form along the fluid, continuous landscape.

Stone is entailed both as a material for emotional response, and a natural language for gaps and caves, reclining upon or intersecting with the sweeping landscape. Shenzhen Bay Cultural Park embraces two transcendental scales of time—the "ancient" and the "future." It provides an alternative experience for citizens at the edge of city, awaking their inherent desire to embrace nature and indulge in cosmic reverie. It manifests a visionary concept of "land art" that evokes temporalities through physical forms.

In 2014, American film director George Lucas initiated an international competition for the design of a new museum of narrative art, which was to be located in Chicago, Illinois, a city rich in American architectural history. MAD's winning design was chosen for its innovative approach and the firm's keen ability to connect the museum with the city's waterfront and surrounding buildings—a vision of architecture-as-landscape. Communicating with the sky, the museum was not conceived as an isolated object, but rather as a spatial experience defined by the people who would occupy and interact with it. However, in 2015, due to controversy over the use of the site, it was decided that the museum would move to a location in California. Los Angeles and San Francisco each bid to be home to this significant cultural asset.

Los Angeles was touted for its status as a hub of cultural activity, one of the most dynamic cities in the United States, and a place that embraces openness. This is not only represented by its diverse cultural demographic, but also through the new architecture that has been emerging in the city from local and international firms. It is a place deeply embedded in the arts, with creative innovation ingrained in its urban fabric.

Thus, in 2015, Los Angeles was selected as the future home to the Lucas Museum of Narrative Art. Located in the city's Exposition Park, a major cultural hub, the museum's building was designed to have a dialogue with both its cultural and residential surroundings and will resemble the canopy of a tree that hovers along the horizon. Situated on 11 acres of new green park space, the museum's 300,000-square-foot building will create a harmonious dialogue with the urban scenery of Los Angeles.

Currently under construction, the five-story museum building will include approximately 100,000 square feet of gallery space, two state-of-the-art cinematic theaters, a library, and numerous spaces for onsite education, as well as restaurants, retail, and event space. A top-level terrace will include paths that meander around a rooftop garden—a kind of floating park with views of the city.

lucas museum of narrative art

As a groundbreaking institution dedicated to the narrative form, the Lucas Museum deserved a state-of-the-art building that is in itself an enduring work of art. Surrounded by more than 500 schools within a five-mile radius, one of the country's leading universities, and three world-class museums, the museum will inspire current and future generations through the universal art of visual storytelling. The building's fluid architecture and new park space will help the institution create meaningful connections with the surrounding community and make a long-lasting impression on the greater city of Los Angeles and the world.

Built to preserve and exhibit local cultural heritage in a context of rapid urbanization, the Ordos Museum is an amorphous building that resembles a polished stone carved out of the Gobi Desert. The monolithic entity, with its surrounding dunes, stairways, and belvederes, shares a similar language with the desert, while it also seems to be willfully alienated from the modern cityscape. It was designed to perform as a critical point in the city center, pointing toward both past and future.

A few years prior to the project commission, Ordos in Inner Mongolia was an outpost in the extensive Gobi Desert. With an economic boom and rapid urbanization, numerous construction projects advanced on the bare land. In 2005, local bureaucrats established a master plan for future development, and the Ordos Museum is considered the centerpiece of the new city.

When MAD received the commission, the project site was still a barren wasteland that posed a sharp contrast to the local government's bold imagination of the future. The tension between reality and ambition reminds Ma Yansong of Buckminster Fuller's famous Manhattan dome, which inspired the design of the Ordos Museum as a tent isolated from the rapidly changing urban environment.

The Ordos Museum has a footprint of 43,000 square meters (462,850 square feet), with one floor below grade and four floors above. The structure is wrapped in polished metal louvers, which results in a solid, windowless building firmly anchored to the ground. Functionally, the building exterior asserts a defensive strategy against the harsh climate. Metaphorically, it is a gesture saluting the disappearing landscape, which has been supplanted by new cityscape.

On entering, the spatial logic alters. An airy monumental cave bathed in sunlight is carved out by the two main exhibition halls. Visitors circulate through the skylit space along the base of sculpted walls and across suspended tectonic bridges, which provide picturesque views of the interior. The passage through canyons and caves echoes with the experience of moving between past and future.

The base of the central canyon connects the two public entries at opposite ends as a through-route. The raised platform with a gentle slope has become a popular gathering space for locals to explore, play, and lounge. A welcoming and respectful attitude makes the design distinct in a time of lofty landmarks.

Since its completion in 2011, the Ordos Museum has played an important role in preserving local cultural heritage and carrying the past forward into contemporary life.

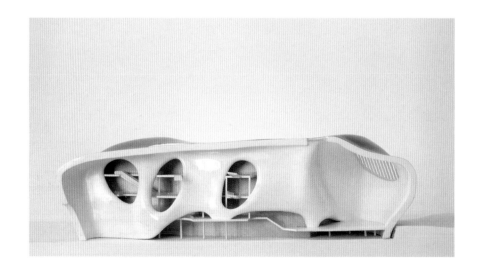

ordos museum

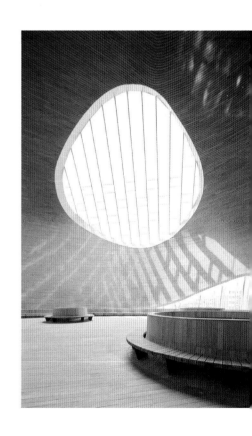

Located in the coastal city of Xiamen, Xinhee Design Center is a corporate complex for the international fashion group Xinhee and its six subsidiary brands. The building is envisioned as a living system with a skin-and-bone structure that explores a reciprocal relationship between interior and exterior.

As the largest fashion brand in Xiamen, Xinhee needed a flexible and efficient work space to energize its creative process. Therefore, the design privileged an innovative workplace that eliminates barriers not only between departments but also between people and the surrounding environment.

The project has a total built area of 61,000 square meters (656,600 square feet) on a site of 15,000 square meters (161,500 square feet). It has a star-shaped layout that spins out six organic arms or branches from the central atrium. A semitransparent PTFE [polytetrafluoroethylene] envelope veils the exterior at a slight distance, also acting as sunshade to diffuse light and provide ventilation to the building during the hot season. The lightweight skin gives the building an elegant and floating appearance, despite its intrinsically logical central bone structure.

Serving as the core of the public space, the atrium is marked by a lush garden and water features. Its openness visually connects different levels and fosters a flexible environment where the various departments can interact. The footbridge across the atrium provides air circulation while also doubling as a catwalk for occasional fashion shows. Living walls and gardens, interlaced with work areas, make up each arm of the star, carrying the energy yet smoothing arrival of nature in the workplace.

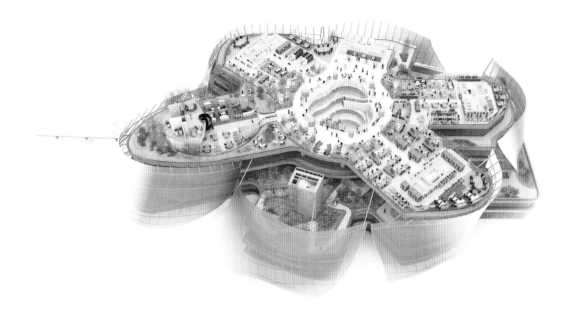

The climate of Xiamen is subtropical, thus the loose relation between skin and bones also makes the building highly efficient. The void and lifted structure on the first floor creates a garden area with water that is accessible to the public. Both the atrium and the distanced envelope enable ventilation through the building during the summer. To lower solar gain and provide natural lighting to the offices, a translucent coating was applied to the building's facade; this permits transmission of 40 percent of light.

MAD believes that architecture should have the ability to serve its users on a much more meaningful level beyond responding to immediate needs. By providing a flexible working environment, Xinhee Design Center seeks to energize its users through its convivial and "breathable" design.

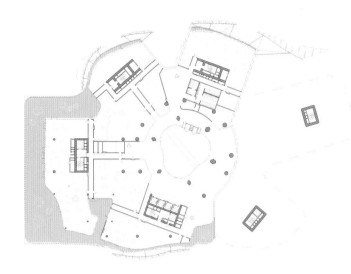

First-Floor Plan

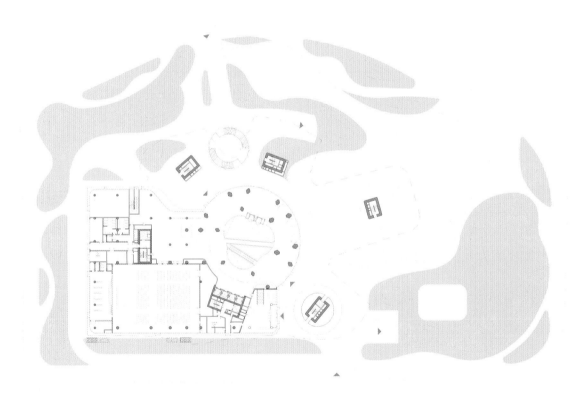

Ground-Floor Plan

0   20   40   60   100m   ◯—N

xinhee design center

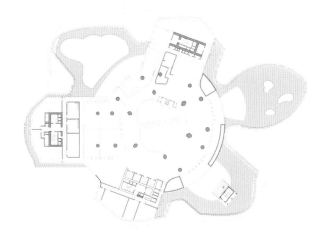

Ninth-Floor Plan

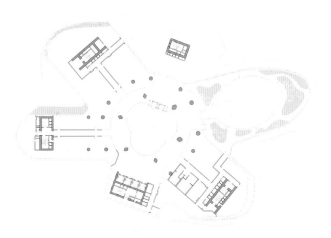

Seventh-Floor Plan

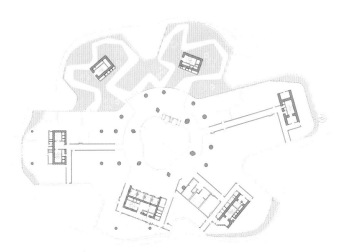

Fifth-Floor Plan

chromatic harmony

Embedded within Harbin's wetlands, the Harbin Opera House is an abstraction of its natural surroundings. Inspired by the powerful aura of the Songhua River, it responds to the force and spirit of the northern Chinese city's untamed wilderness, frigid climate, and rich musical history.

The northern bank of the Songhua River used to be a stark boundary between city and nature, where expanded wetlands form a unique yet isolated topography. As more people have come to work and live there in the course of urban expansion, the Harbin Cultural Island master plan was devised in response to a rising demand for cultural life. Harbin Opera House is the focal point of the master plan, which also consists of a cultural center and the surrounding landscape.

harbin opera house

As the birthplace of China's first symphony orchestra, Harbin has a long musical tradition. The rise and fall of the Songhua River creates a natural rhythm along its bank. Embracing musicality and the sinuous landscape, the architecture is wrapped by a curvilinear facade composed of smooth white aluminum panels, evoking the idea of poetry made up of edge and surface, softness and sharpness.

Harbin Opera House has a building area of 79,000 square meters (850,000 square feet) on a 72,000-square-meter (775,000-square-foot) site. It features a grand theater that seats 1,600 people and a smaller theater that can hold an audience of 400. The architectural procession choreographs a conceptual narrative that transforms visitors into performers. The journey begins upon crossing the bridge onto Harbin Cultural Island, where the undulating architectural mass wraps a large public plaza and, during winter months, melts into the snowy environment. Upon entering the grand lobby, visitors encounter a large transparent glass curtain wall that spans the space, visually connecting the warm curvilinear wooden interior with the swooping facade and exterior plaza. A glass wall supported by a lightweight diagrid structure soars over the grand lobby, where the audience is greeted with the simple opulence of natural light and materials.

Warm and inviting, the grand theater emulates a wooden block that has been gently eroded. It is clad with bent narrow planks of Manchurian ash from the proscenium to the mezzanine balcony, and the design integrates theater systems to create world-class acoustics. Within the second, smaller theater, the interior is connected seamlessly to the exterior by a large panoramic window behind the performance stage. This wall of soundproof glass provides a natural scenic backdrop for performances and activates the stage as an extension of the outdoor environment, inspiring production opportunities.

harbin opera house

Harbin Opera House emphasizes public interaction and participation with the building. At the apex, visitors discover an open performance space that serves as an observation platform and offers panoramic views of Harbin's skyline and the wetlands below. Upon descent, visitors return to the expansive public plaza, which can also be used as an event space for locals to relax and lounge in.

harbin opera house

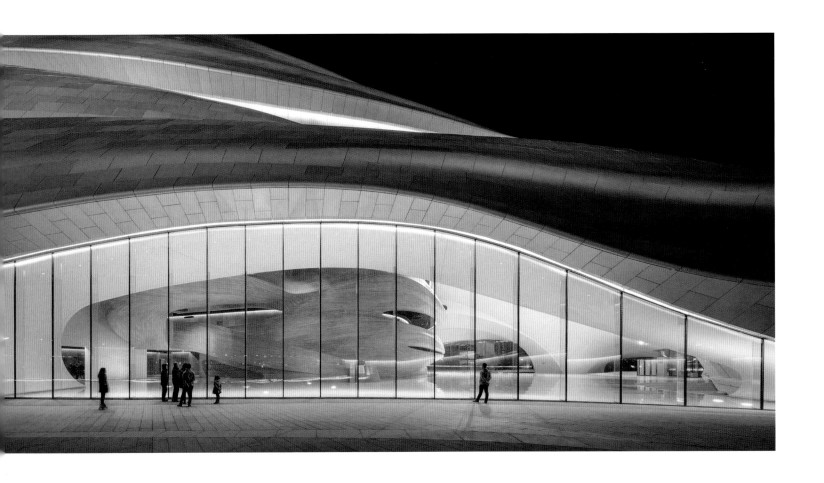

harbin opera house

Completed in 2015, Harbin Opera House has held over 1,000 performances. It is now seen as a cultural center of the city—a dynamic performance venue, as well as a dramatic public space that brings unique natural scenery into the cultural life of citizens.

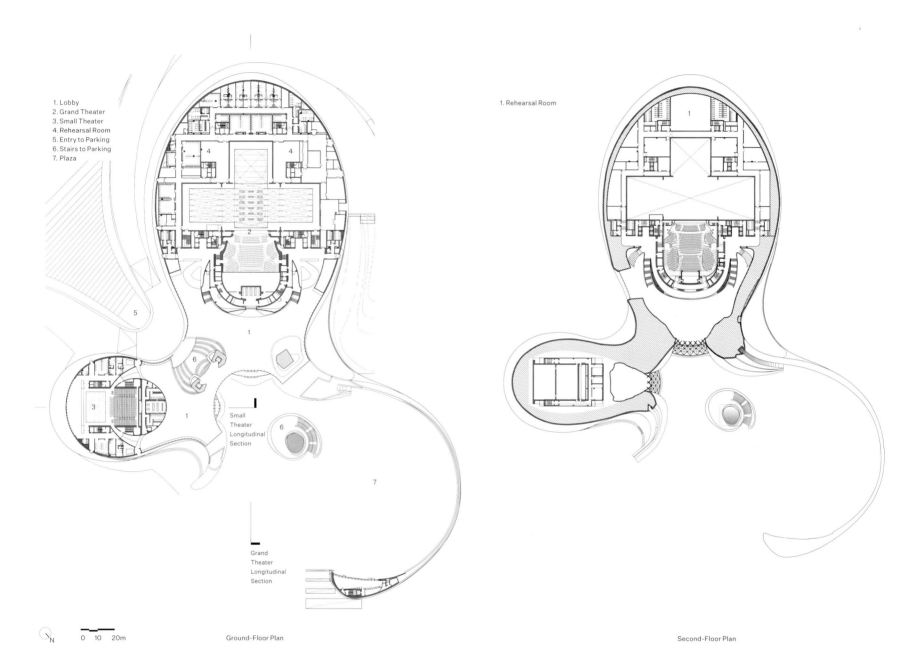

1. Lobby
2. Grand Theater
3. Small Theater
4. Rehearsal Room
5. Entry to Parking
6. Stairs to Parking
7. Plaza

1. Rehearsal Room

Small
Theater
Longitudinal
Section

Grand
Theater
Longitudinal
Section

N

0   10   20m

Ground-Floor Plan

Second-Floor Plan

harbin opera house

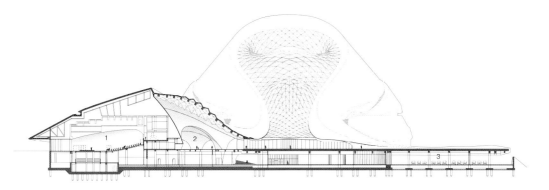

1. Small Theater
2. Lobby
3. Parking

Small Theater Longitudinal Section

0 5 10   20m

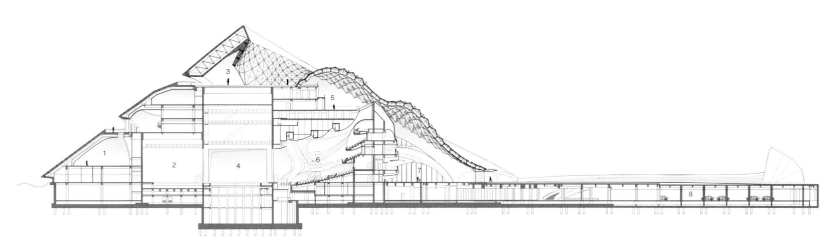

1. Rehearsal Room
2. Backstage
3. Rooftop
4. Main Stage

5. Roof Garden
6. Seating
7. Lobby
8. Parking

Grand Theater Longitudinal Section

0 5 10   20m

chaoyang park plaza 2017 / Beijing, China

Located in the central business district of Beijing, Chaoyang Park Plaza is a multiuse office, commercial, and residential complex that unfolds like a classic *shan shui* painting on an urban scale. The form of the architectural complex is found in nature but is conveyed through a kind of sophisticated artificiality that breaks the binary view of the natural and manmade worlds. The project raises doubts about the generic modern city and suggests another possibility of nature expressed through and in the built environment.

The complex is located on the southern edge of Chaoyang Park, the largest remaining park in the central business district. Since 2008, the skyline of Beijing has morphed rapidly with the addition of a series of modernist buildings. The location of Chaoyang Park Plaza places the design in a position of conversation with the idyllic urban park and a district of skyscrapers.

The idea of MAD was to naturalize the strong artificial skyline of the district by borrowing scenery from a distant landscape, a classical approach to Chinese gardens, where nature is evoked through relationships, poetic imagery, and the extension of nature. The design introduces natural forms and spaces—mountain, brook, creek, rocks, valley, and forest—into the city, remodeling the relationship of large-scale architecture within the urban center.

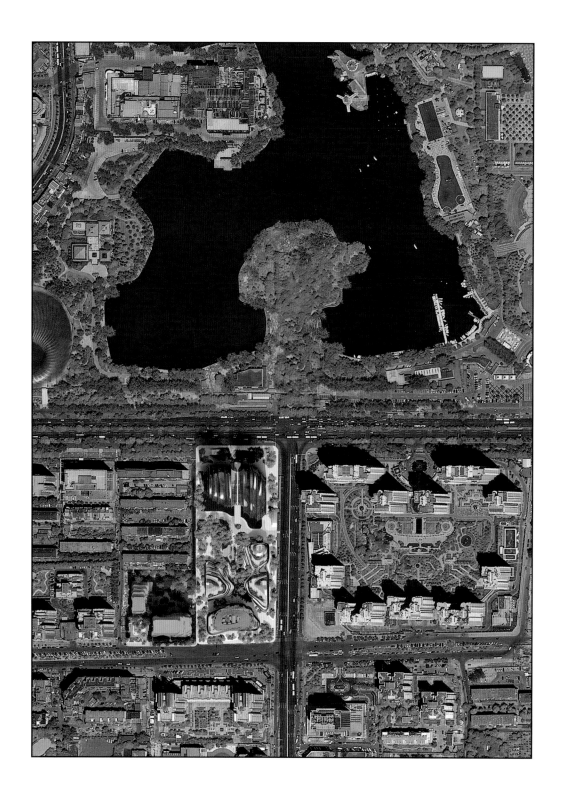

chaoyang park plaza

The 220,000-square-meter (2,368,000-square-foot) complex includes ten buildings of various scales. On the northern side of the complex, asymmetrical twin tower office buildings sit at the base of the lake and resemble two mountain peaks rising out of the water. The transparent and bright atrium acts as a drawstring that pulls the two towers together with a continuous glass rooftop structure.

chaoyang park plaza

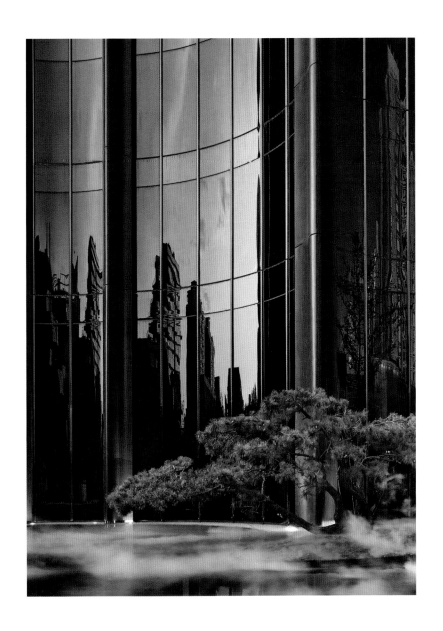

Located to the south of the towers, four low-rise commercial buildings are shaped like river stones that have been eroded over time. Seemingly random, their strategic relationship to one another forms a secluded yet open urban garden, offering a place for people to meet in a natural setting in the midst of the city. Adjacent to the office buildings are two multi-level residential buildings in the southwest area of the complex. These buildings continue the mid-air courtyard concept and provide all who live there with the freedom to wander through an urban forest.

The project has received LEED Gold Certification, confirming that the ideal of nature is embodied not only in the design concept, but through the integration of green technology as well. Vertical fins in the design also function as the ventilation and filtration system, drawing fresh air indoors. At the base of the towers, a series of ponds works as a cooling system in the summer, moderating interior temperature.

chaoyang park plaza

Chaoyang Park Plaza shifts the paradigm of architecture typically found in central business districts. By exploring the symbiotic relationship between modern urban architecture and the natural environment, it revives the harmonious coexistence of urban life and nature. It creates a *shan shui* city where people can share their individual emotions and a sense of belonging.

chaoyang park plaza

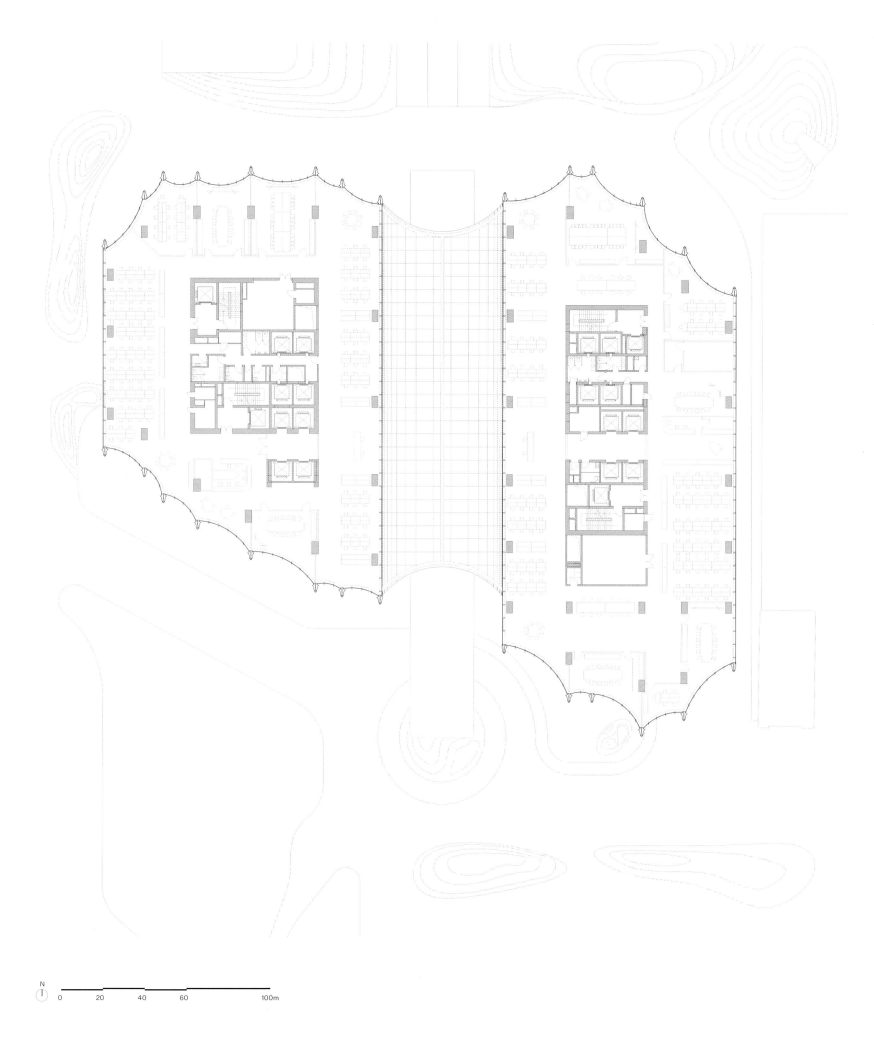

chaoyang park plaza

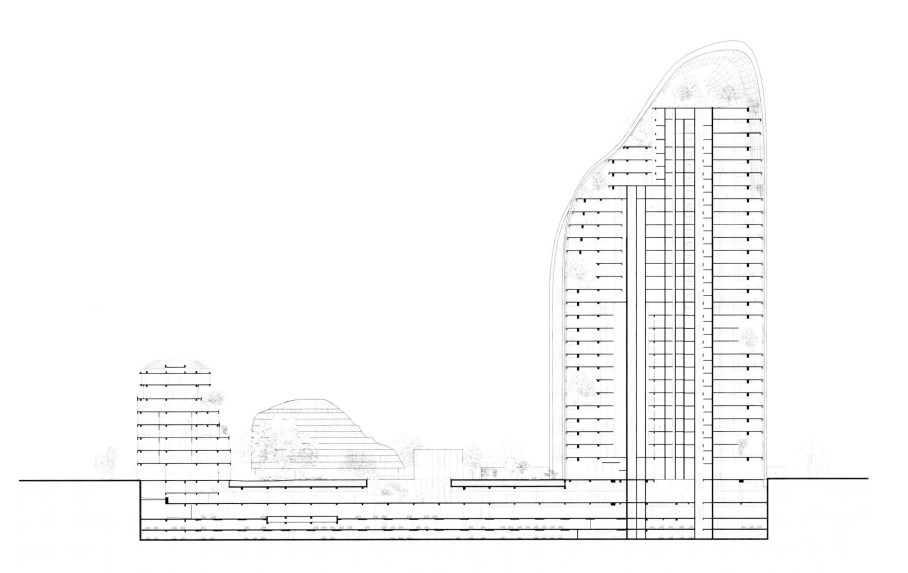

0   20   40   60   100m

The Nanjing Zendai Himalayas Center is a metropolis-scale development consisting of commercial, hotel, office, and residential functions. The development seeks to restore the spiritual harmony between people and nature by integrating contemplative spaces and immersing residents in nature while still meeting the demands of modern living.

Founded over 2,600 years ago, Nanjing is a historic city with deep cultural heritage that has become highly modernized. Having served as the capital of several Chinese dynasties, Nanjing still holds a prominent place in the nation's culture scene. Flourishing both culturally and architecturally, it enjoys a tapestry of natural and historical landscapes—mountains, water, palaces, temples—as its backdrop.

nanjing zendai himalayas center

Over the past decade, Nanjing has gradually evolved from its original cultural context to become home to one of the country's largest railway stations, which spurred numerous large-scale constructions that form a new district of Nanjing. Among them is the six-city-block development, the Zendai Himalayas Center.

With two points of focus, historical heritage, and a high degree of modernization, MAD strives to achieve a balance between the city's historic past and its high-tech future. The complex, covering 560,000 square meters (6,028,000 square feet), is composed of six lots, two of which are linked by a vertical city plaza. Thirteen mountainous towers stand along the perimeter of the village. Curved ascending corridors and paths weave through the undulating commercial complexes, bringing people from the busy ground level to the vertical park, where they enjoy opportunities to wander among the buildings and gardens.

nanjing zendai himalayas center

The design is envisaged within the traditional Chinese ethos of *shan shui* (mountain and river)—a painting style as well as a vehicle for Chinese philosophy—albeit in a modern setting. The mountainous towers on the edge of the complex are characterized by vertical sun shading and white curved glass screens that flow like waterfalls. These features provide interior spaces with ample light and breeze, generating a subtle and calm ambience. Meandering through the towers, water features, such as ponds, waterfalls, brooks, and pools, connect buildings and landscapes, integrating the different elements. This integration goes beyond form, as the water features also function as reservoirs to collect and recycle rainwater for irrigation.

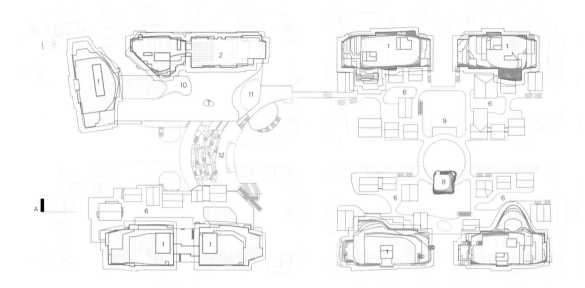
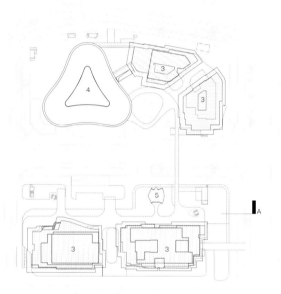

Site Plan

1. Office	7. Shopping Mall
2. Loft Apartment	8. Flagship Store
3. Apartment	9. Outdoor Theater
4. Hotel	10. Roof Garden
5. Elevator Tower	11. Plaza
6. Commercial Village	12. Urban Bridge

nanjing zendai himalayas center

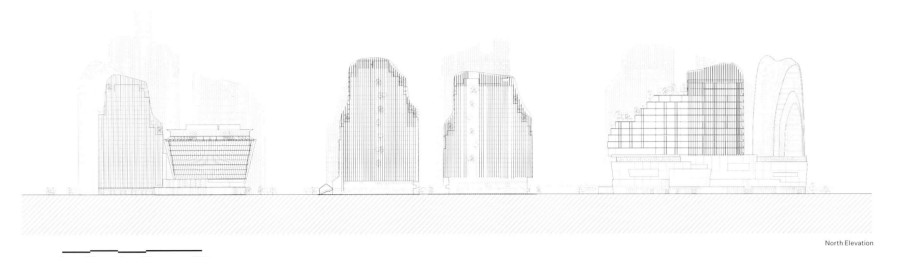

North Elevation

0   20   40   60   100m

Section A–A

0   20   40   60   100m

nanjing zendai himalayas center

At the center of the complex, there is a village like community of low-rise buildings connected by footbridges and nestled into the landscape. This scene of footbridges, artificial hills, and flowing water creates a poetic environment at the heart of the project. By activating green valleys, the design offers an approachable landscape that permits the human scale to mediate with the large size of the buildings.

The Nanjing Zendai Himalayas Center was completed in 2021. By building a symbiotic relationship between inhabitants and their dwelling environment, the complex brings together the cultural spirit of a historic city and its modern needs.

Located in Beverly Hills, Gardenhouse is a mixed-use scheme consisting of varied housing typologies above ground-floor commercial space. Peeking above the landscaped envelope, a cluster of white-facade gabled-roof structures with irregularly shaped windows creates a dynamic neighborhood. It is a playful, witty, though simple homage to the iconic hillsides of Los Angeles. It brings a new dynamic to Los Angeles by rethinking the role of residential architecture and its ability to foster interpersonal interactions.

gardenhouse

Gardenhouse was envisioned as a hillside village in which the architecture acts as the hill. With eighteen units of different housing types, the 4,460-square-meter (48,000-square-foot) structure introduced a mixture of residential typologies that was previously unavailable in Beverly Hills. With the largest living green wall in the United States, it is covered in lush plantings of native, drought-tolerant succulents and vines whose familiarity with the local climate negates the need for extra irrigation and maintenance. The result is a unique texture forming an organic, natural, seasonal addition to the neighborhood streetscape.

Inspired by the natural surroundings of the Los Angeles foothills, Gardenhouse has been designed as a continuation of the existing landscape. At ground level, residents are welcomed by a grotto like space that serves as a quiet and serene oasis, with a water feature at the heart of the project. Further ahead, the softness of the cave meets a bright conclusion, with natural light flooding through a connected water feature from the courtyard patio above.

gardenhouse

The healthy mixture of typologies and living green walls results in a sense of community while maintaining a feeling of individuality and exclusiveness as well. With careful consideration given to the distance, orientation, and arrangement, each dwelling features a balcony that extends individual space to overlook the central courtyard. This allows inhabitants to interact with each other across the courtyard and cultivates the feeling of a private neighborhood. At the same time, each unit maintains its own independent circulation route, and interior expressions are all different under pitch-roof volume.

gardenhouse

Through Gardenhouse, MAD seeks to offer a rebuttal to the stereotypical cubic-box living environments of high-density cities across the world. An intrinsic connection with nature, with a tranquil, shared courtyard and private outdoor space for each unit, shapes a calm oasis just steps away from the urban environment. It creates possibilities for community building in the modern city, raising awareness of sharing in public life.

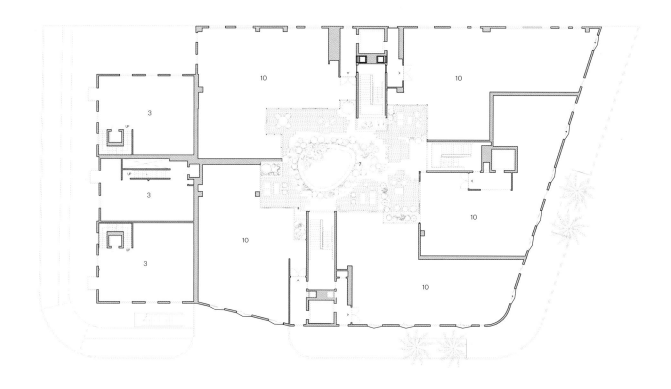

Second-Floor Plan

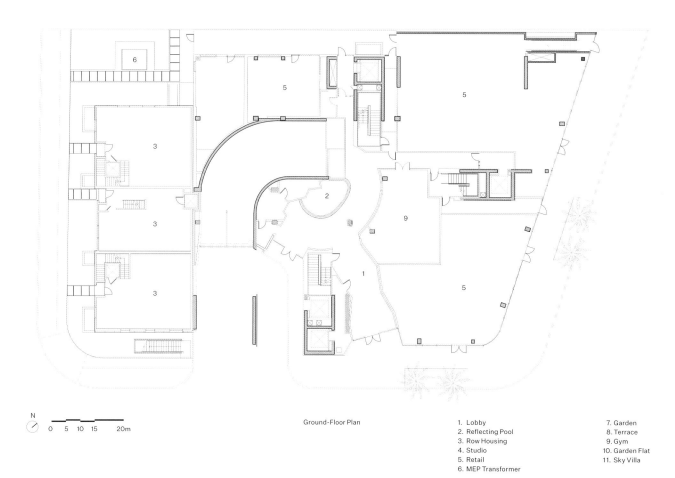

N

0 5 10 15   20m

Ground-Floor Plan

1. Lobby
2. Reflecting Pool
3. Row Housing
4. Studio
5. Retail
6. MEP Transformer

7. Garden
8. Terrace
9. Gym
10. Garden Flat
11. Sky Villa

gardenhouse

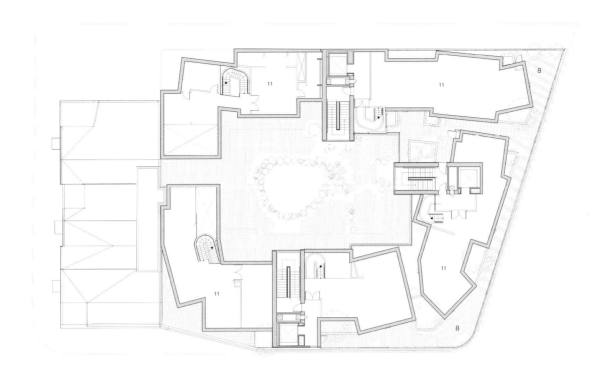

Fourth-Floor Plan

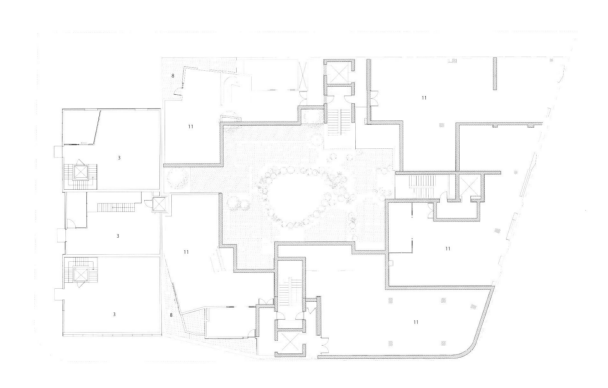

N

0   5   10 15   20m

Third-Floor Plan

1. Lobby
2. Reflecting Pool
3. Row Housing
4. Studio
5. Retail
6. MEP Transformer

7. Garden
8. Terrace
9. Gym
10. Garden Flat
11. Sky Villa

UNIC is a residential building that emerges from Clichy-Batignolles, a mixed-use eco-district in the seventeenth arrondissement of Paris. Created in the context of an urban master plan, it seeks to connect and enrich the surrounding communities by mixing socioeconomic classes and generations, bringing nature to the city, enhancing public spaces with improved mobility, and promoting renewable energy sources.

The neighborhood reactivation plan for Clichy-Batignolles includes large-scale construction of different types of housing that are connected through shared facilities, such as schools, retail, recreational areas, and other community resources. Unlike traditional residential housing, the design by MAD takes on an organic shape to weave nature into the urban fabric.

Facing the ten-hectare green space of Martin Luther King Park, UNIC enjoys abundant natural space in the neighborhood. Accentuated by sinuous floor plates, each asymmetrical level slightly tapers as the building ascends to create dynamic spaces inside. The floating and ascending form also seeks to offer organic spaces for residents. The design attempts to blur the boundary between architecture and nature through variably stepped terraces, which extend the green areas into the vertical space while providing room for residents to interact with nature.

In a city where high-rise construction had not been the norm, the thirteen-story building will not tip the scale, but it does provide beautiful panoramic views, including that of the Eiffel Tower. The lightness of the materiality complements the free-flowing curves of the structure. The building employs a simple double-core structure and bare concrete facade, both of which showcase the design's elegance and simplicity. Its podium is conjoined with an adjacent public housing project and provides direct access to the Métro infrastructure and community resources, including a kindergarten, retail spaces, and restaurants. The design enhances everyday community relations in a diverse socioeconomic neighborhood.

After winning a design competition, MAD worked closely with the local government, city planners, and local architects in a series of workshops to explore topics from macro-scale urban plans to micro-scale details, such as sustainable community development, resource sharing, energy management, and population demographics. UNIC was the result of these workshops with developers, architects, and residents of Clichy-Batignolles.

Embracing the Parisian legacy of gardens while meeting current socioeconomic needs, UNIC actively enhances its relationship with the community, represents the neighborhood's evolution, and offers a vision of how nature can be integrated into high-density living in urban environments in the future.

N

0   5   10   20m   Fourth-Floor Plan

Jiaxing Civic Center is located close to Nanhu Lake and the central axis of the city of Jiaxing in Zhejiang Province. Jiaxing is a city of 4.5 million people on the Jing-Hang Grand Canal. The complex consists of a science and technology hall, an activity center for women and children, and a youth activity center. Thanks to the unique historical significance of Jiaxing, this public building embodies multiple layers of meaning.

MAD envisions municipal public architecture that enhances a sense of community and cohesion. Therefore, the master plan, with a footprint of 130,000 square meters (1.4 million square feet), links three functional venues hand-in-hand in a circular shape connected by a roof. The enclosed terrace, roof garden, central green space, landscape corridor, and outdoor theater are integrated into a whole, turning the complex into a vibrant courtyard for the city. The circular courtyard of the complex itself counters the subdued mood commonly generated by large complexes.

The exterior of the architecture above the water is covered by white ceramic panels that echo elegant yet modest typical Jiangnan roof tiles. The flowing roof resembles a ribbon in the wind, but when seen from above appears like a whirlpool amid calm water. These images correspond to the tranquility and flowing movements of this town on the water. The second-level platform is the focal point of the complex. A landscape corridor and a 350-meter (1,150-foot) track compose the central ring corridor, where people can walk along the gentle slope to the central green space on the ground floor. Visitors can also climb up to the exterior terrace, or to the landscaped forest area outside the complex. Because the boundaries of programs are not delineated, the exhibition hall, theater, education space, activity space, parent-child center, interactive entertainment area, and other functions are organically combined to complement one another.

The central green space on the ground floor is not only a place for people to rest and play, but also an open plaza where large-scale cultural activities can be staged. The architecture retreats from the inner courtyard, while the exterior and interior are separated by full-height glazing that forms varied semi-outdoor terraces and roof gardens, which are also excellent sightseeing platforms.

Upon completion, Jiaxing Civic Center is expected to become a cultural landmark that provides a natural, egalitarian, and accessible open space. The embracing courtyard carves out room for community in a city where life moves at a fast pace.

Second-Floor Plan

1. Lobby
2. Gallery
3. Multifunction Hall
4. Dome Theater
5. Classroom
6. Youth Theater
7. Gala Hall
8. Children's Zone
9. Sports & Entertainment Area
10. Lecture Hall
11. Family Interaction Area
12. Family Education Area
13. Reserved Area
14. Sunken Garden
15. Amphitheater
16. Sunken Plaza
17. Lift to 2F Terrace
18. Stair to 2F Terrace
19. Drop-Off
20. Lake
21. Central Green Plaza
22. Office
23. Culture and Art Exhibition
24. Childhood Experience Area
25. Health Promotion Area
26. Practical Experience Area
27. Void
28. Terrace
29. National Art Area
30. Quality Improvement Area
31. Parking
32. Parking Entrance

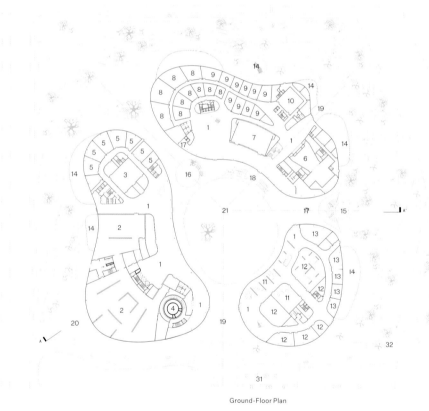

Ground-Floor Plan

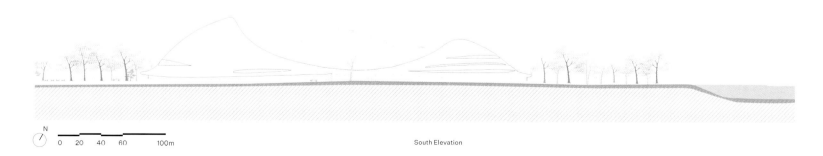

N

0   20   40   60   100m

South Elevation

jiaxing civic center

Roof Plan

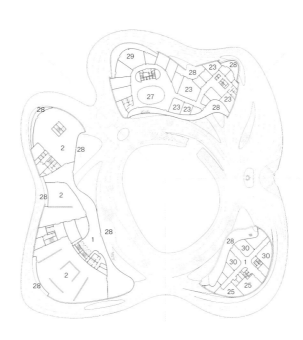

Third-Floor Plan

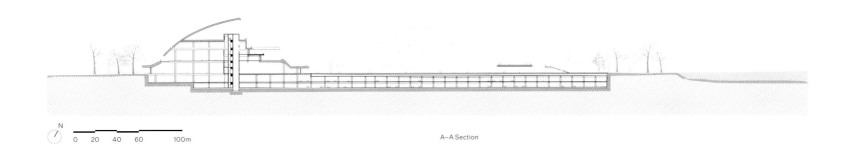

N

0   20   40   60   100m

A–A Section

elemental landscape

In 2000, the Echigo-Tsumari Art Triennale was founded with the intention of using art and culture to reinvigorate the Echigo-Tsumari area of Japan, which suffers from economic contraction and is home to an aging population. For the event, numerous art installations by local and internationally renowned artists were dispersed through the region's fields, forests, schools, empty houses, and abandoned spaces. These projects enrich the area and have become an integral part of the local community.

Opened in 2018 as part of the festival, Tunnel of Light was designed to restore the Kiyotsu Gorge Tunnel in Niigata prefecture, transforming the historic lookout tunnel into a trail of artistic spaces. It cuts through 750 meters (2,460 feet) of rock formations and offers a panoramic view across one of Japan's largest canyons.

The Tunnel of Light restored the historic tunnel and the sightseeing platform through the realization of several architectural and artistic spaces.

The minimalistic design strategies employ lighting and natural forces to create an environment in which the illusory and the real overlap. Technical sophistication gives way to the raw and natural presence of mountain and sky.

tunnel of light

トンネル

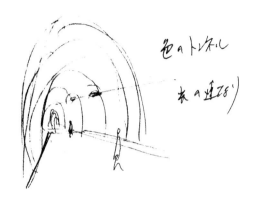

色のトンネル

表の速さり

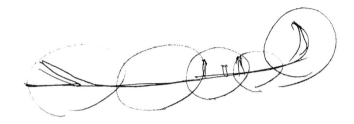

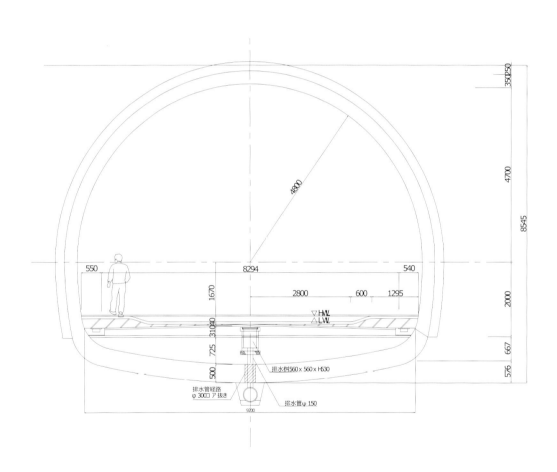

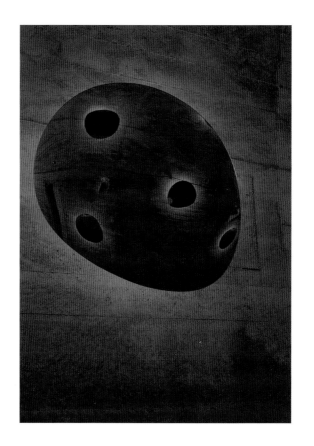

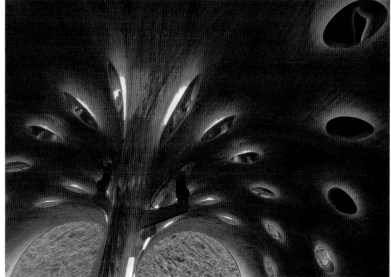

tunnel of light

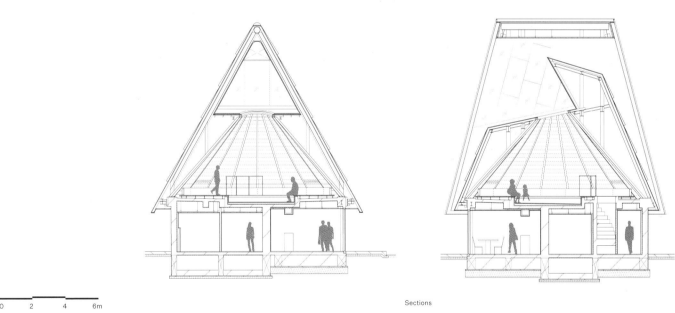

Sections

0   2   4   6m

Periscope, Expression of Color, Invisible Bubble, Drop, and Light Cave chart a journey through the tunnel. On the approach to the tunnel there is a small wooden hut that features an opening in its pitched cedar roof called the "periscope." Visitors can enjoy the natural scenery through the periscope from the comfort of the spa inside the warm wooden interior. The entrance to the tunnel sees a renovated passageway illuminated by a series of colored lights, each defining a lookout point along the tunnel. Described as the "expression" of the space, it combines the vibrancy of the colors with mysterious music to create a dynamic ambiance that sparks curiosity about the unknown in visitors. The installation seeks to bring new perspectives to the space and to provide a spiritual sense of reflection, relaxation, contemplation, and introspection. Tunnel of Light allows visitors to transcend the role of observer and to become active participants. It allows individuals to place themselves in nature in unexpected ways.

In 2018 alone, the Tunnel of Light attracted more than 180,000 visitors, triple the number seen in 2017. The boom in tourism has revived the region's economy. In 2019, the Japan Arts Council selected the Tunnel of Light as one of five works it believes exemplify the rich scope of the country's arts and culture on a global level.

In 2017, MAD Architects was commissioned by the Yabuli China Entrepreneurs Forum (CEF), one of China's most influential business organizations, to design and build a permanent venue for its annual summits, a landmark that would reflect the members' entrepreneurial spirit. The conference center is located in the snow-covered mountains of northeastern China, known for rugged terrain and frigid temperatures.

yabuli entrepreneurs' congress center

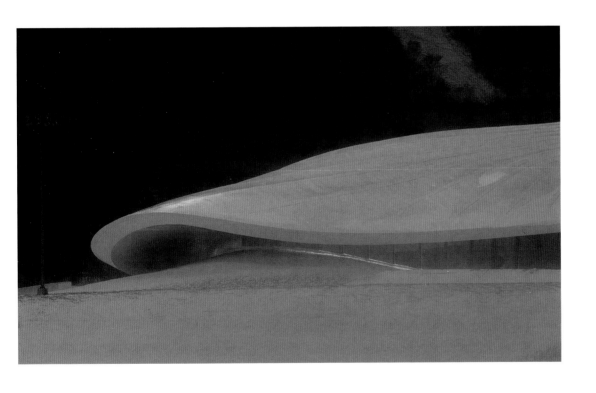

MAD's scheme rests on the concept of a tent sitting at the foot of a mountain, with its soft, curving, silver-white rooftop echoing the snow-capped hills surrounding it. During the day, natural light floods the internal spaces through a giant glass skylight. At night, the same sky-light allows the building to emit a warm glow into the cold mountain forest, evoking the image of a campfire around which entrepreneurs share ideas, thoughts, and stories. Inside, a blend of wooden walls and natural light creates a warm, soft atmosphere, while an outdoor public plaza and glass walkway allow users to marvel and be inspired by the connection between architecture and nature.

yabuli entrepreneurs' congress center

The venue contains an exhibition hall, meeting rooms, and a television hall. Its blend of mixed-use spaces makes it suitable to accommodate large-scale conferences, corporate training, and other events. The venue is also open to the public, with the exhibition hall serving as a valuable tool for showcasing and exploring Chinese entrepreneurship.

Funded and established by fifty Yabuli CEF members, the conference center marks an important milestone in Chinese entrepreneurship and is destined to become a valuable social treasure.

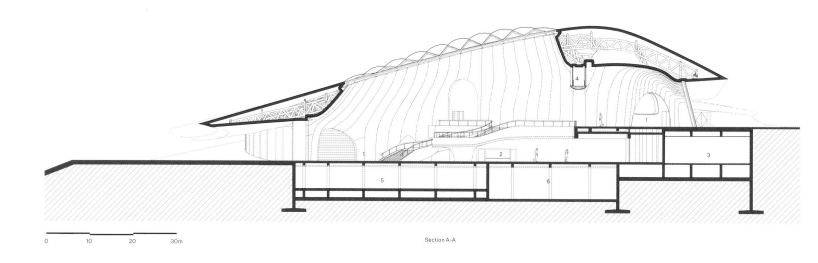

0   10   20   30m   Section A-A

yabuli entrepreneurs' congress center

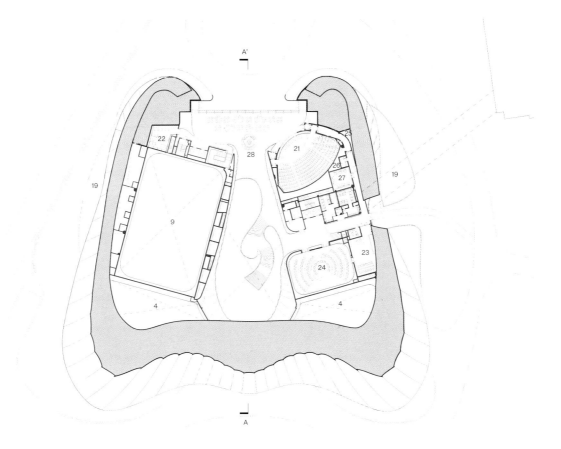

Second-Floor Plan

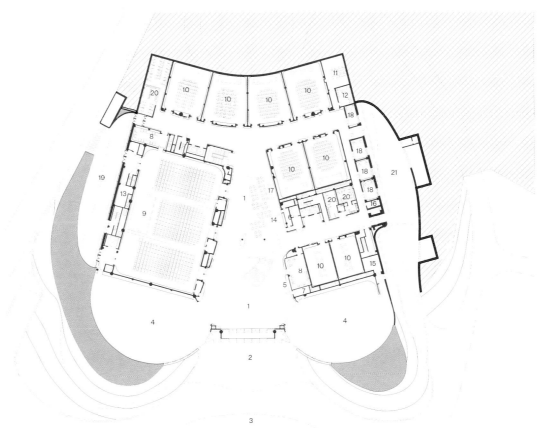

Ground-Floor Plan

1. Lobby
2. Main Entrance
3. Entrance Square
4. Museum
5. Service Counter
6. Service Room
7. Cloakroom
8. VIP Room
9. Taiking Hall
10. Conference Room
11. Office
12. Master Control Room
13. Dressing Room
14. Bar
15. Control Room
16. Duty Room
17. Self-Service Counter
18. Interview Room
19. Sunken Courtyard
20. Bathroom
21. Alibaba Hall
22. Smoking Area
23. Library
24. Council Hall
25. Equipment Room
26. Store
27. Meeting Room
28. 2F Lobby

quzhou sports park

TRAINING CENTER   NATATORIUM   GYMNASIUM   STADIUM   TRACK

Located in Zhejiang province, Quzhou Sports Park manifests as a piece of "land art" that submerges itself into a futuristic landscape of hills, sunken gardens, and a lake. Breaking away from conventional sports complexes that signify progress and power, this project seeks to bring together elite competition among professional athletes with the physical activities of everyday people. The sports spirit is supplemented by an oasis of urban parkland, contributing to the city's cultural life.

Quzhou is a historical city with extensive forestry covering more than 70 percent of its land area. A profound cultural heritage and an abundance of natural resources form the precious wealth and identity of the city. As a continuation of the existing landscape, MAD envisions an otherworldly plan where buildings disappear into the undulating landscape, while the spirit of sport is merged with an embodied knowledge of nature.

The periphery of the site is surrounded by a dense forest that shelters the park from the city, while the design choreographs an excursion from the wider urban context to this otherworldly landscape. The 700,000-square-meter (7,500,000 square feet) sports park consists of a stadium (30,000-person) and a gymnasium (10,000-person), along with a natatorium, sports hall, and outdoor sports venues. The campus also includes a science and technology museum, a hotel, and retail areas.

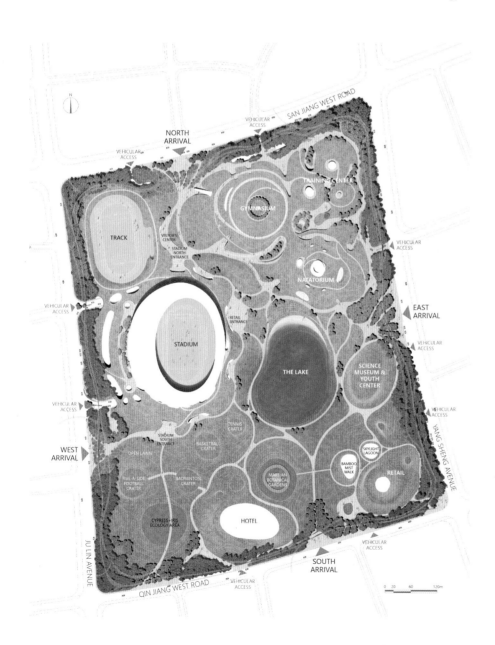

quzhou sports park

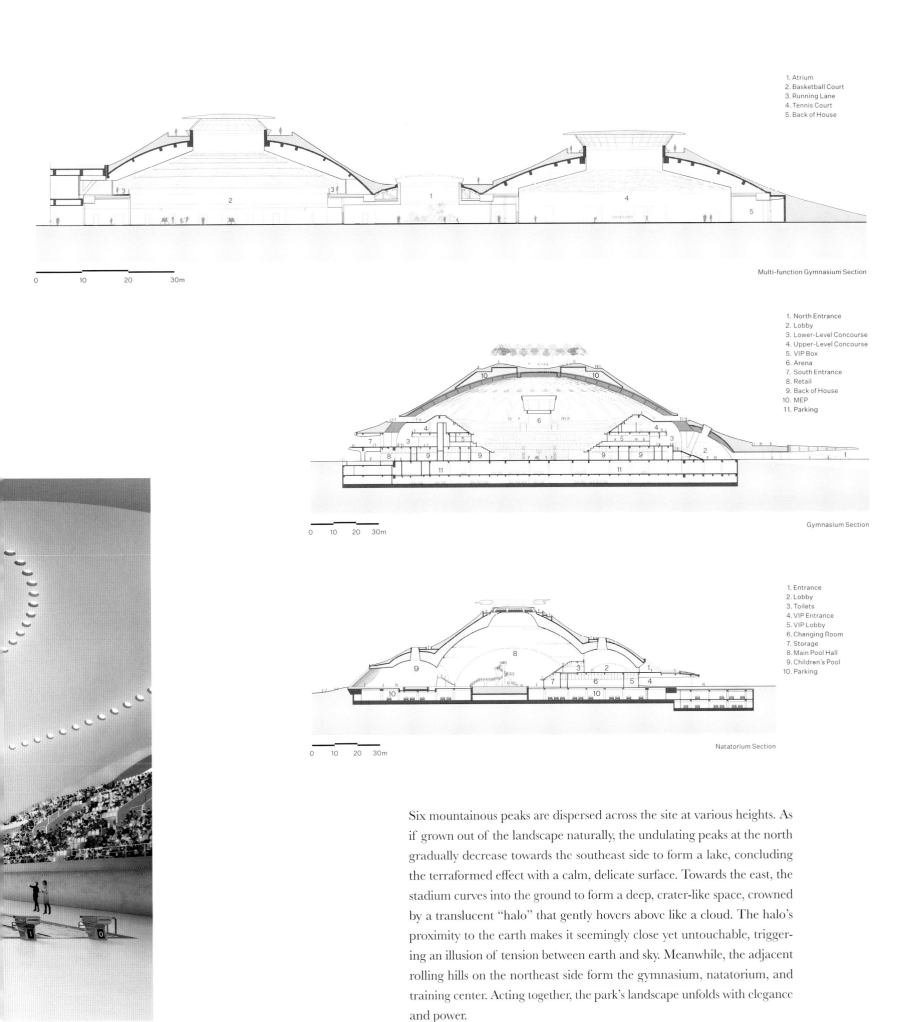

1. Atrium
2. Basketball Court
3. Running Lane
4. Tennis Court
5. Back of House

0   10   20   30m

Multi-function Gymnasium Section

1. North Entrance
2. Lobby
3. Lower-Level Concourse
4. Upper-Level Concourse
5. VIP Box
6. Arena
7. South Entrance
8. Retail
9. Back of House
10. MEP
11. Parking

0   10   20   30m

Gymnasium Section

1. Entrance
2. Lobby
3. Toilets
4. VIP Entrance
5. VIP Lobby
6. Changing Room
7. Storage
8. Main Pool Hall
9. Children's Pool
10. Parking

0   10   20   30m

Natatorium Section

Six mountainous peaks are dispersed across the site at various heights. As if grown out of the landscape naturally, the undulating peaks at the north gradually decrease towards the southeast side to form a lake, concluding the terraformed effect with a calm, delicate surface. Towards the east, the stadium curves into the ground to form a deep, crater-like space, crowned by a translucent "halo" that gently hovers above like a cloud. The halo's proximity to the earth makes it seemingly close yet untouchable, triggering an illusion of tension between earth and sky. Meanwhile, the adjacent rolling hills on the northeast side form the gymnasium, natatorium, and training center. Acting together, the park's landscape unfolds with elegance and power.

Stadium Section

Moving from exterior to interior, the architecture transforms from mountains to caves that open at their top. The natatorium is formed by three hills that create a bubble-like interior. Meanwhile, the gymnasium spans wide over the land, supported by a concrete structure that manifests strength, emphasizes the cavity, and embraces quality emotionally on the interior.

As the focal point of the park, the lake flows naturally along the slope from the north to the southeast side. The massing to the south is composed of a science and technology museum, a hotel, and a retail area, whose program appeals to both teenagers and adult citizens. The mountainous hotel forms a memorable sightseeing platform, offering a panoramic view of the entire park.

quzhou sports park

Contours are engraved into the surface of the site, some of which form pedestrian pathways that weave between the mountains and over the architectural forms. Naturally serving as a new place for citizens to engage in exercise, the organic pathways offer the opportunity for people to "climb" the buildings beneath. The lawn also provides a place where people can relax after their excursions, introducing a new public green space to the city.

The design for this sport park breaks away from that of traditional stadia and athletic complexes which frequently prioritize structural power. The Quzhou Sports Park imagines an alternative scheme where architecture gives way to the landscape. Structural power thus gives way to a physical engagement with ordinary people. Upon completion, the project will become the world's largest earth-sheltered architectural work, inspiring a new type of urban civilization defined by a respect for human emotions.

huangshan mountain village   2016 / Huangshan, China

Mount Huangshan, located near the ancient villages of Hongcun and Xidi in Anhui province, is known for its verdant scenery and distinctive granite peaks. It is a UNESCO World Heritage Site whose beautiful, tranquil environment has become an increasingly popular tourist destination.

The 69,600-square-meter (749,000-square-foot) Huangshan Mountain Village development is part of a larger tourism master plan for Huangshan Taiping Lake, which will provide facilities on a 100-hectare (250-acre) site. While meeting the needs of modern living, the design affirms the significance of this culturally important mountain range. Composed in deference to the local topography, all of the buildings are diverse in height and appearance and have been conceived to ensure that the original mountain heights are echoed. Organized in a linked configuration across the southern shore of the lake, the ten buildings have a dynamic relationship and establish a new type of village landscape: one where architecture becomes nature, and nature dissolves into architecture.

The apartments have been envisioned as quiet retreats. Each one has an expansive balcony whose organic lines respond to the topographic contours of the immediate mountain terrain. With their shapes informed by nearby tea fields, they appear to have been sculpted by wind and water, with no two the same. Each floorplate decreases in scale toward the summit, tapering to create a peaklike formation along the edge of Taiping Lake. Extending the interior to the exterior, the design provides abundant outdoor space, immersing residents in the mountain breezes. Pathways determined by the landscape naturally meander through the trees and between the buildings, offering unique access to the site.

huangshan mountain village

The village appears to have grown organically out of
the sinuous landscape. It offers a new type of vertical living that, while architecturally complementing
the surrounding forest, also enhances the comfort
and emotional well-being of residents. The poetic
vision of *shan shui* (mountain and river) is not, strictly
speaking, an imitation of natural forms, but it evokes
synergy among people, local culture, and nature.

Located on the south bank of the Dongyang River, the Yiwu Grand Theater consists of two theaters and a conference center, alongside a large plaza. The form of the architecture brings to mind a boat sailing on the river, responding to the cultural heritage and future expectations of the city and region.

Yiwu, in China's Zhejiang province, has established itself internationally with its strong economy, based on the largest wholesale commodities market in the world. The history of the city and its cultural heritage can be traced back to the Qin dynasty (221–206 B.C.E.). Now, as an integral part of the country's Belt and Road Initiative, the city needs to present a more rounded image with an important place for culture, hence the creation of the Yiwu Grand Theater.

Positioned with mountains as a distant backdrop and water as its stage, the theater is defined by a layering of glass sails that are reminiscent of the Chinese junks that once transported goods. The curves of the architecture also echo the Jiangnan-style eaves of the ancient vernacular architecture of the region. The transparency and lightness of the glass bring to mind the texture of a thin, silky fabric, creating a dynamic rhythm that makes these "sails" appear as if they are blowing in the wind.

The Yiwu Grand Theater encompasses a large (1,600-seat) theater, a medium (1,200-seat) theater, and an international conference center (for 2,000 people). Visitors can enter the complex from the main entrance at ground level, or from the central "valley" at the deck level. Because of the translucent facade, the interior is bathed in sunlight. The fabriclike canopies act not only as an envelope around the building, but also as a shading system that optimizes the use of natural light inside. Views of the lush surrounding landscape are visible from the interiors. At the heart of the project is a screen with a water feature that animates the space and engages audiences before they enter the theaters.

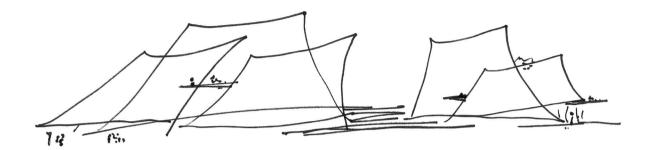

The concept of floating is enhanced by integration of materials, lighting, and acoustic design. The seating areas bring to mind vessels floating on the water. Organically shaped translucent panels resembling soft fabric compose the ceiling and walls. They veil a lighting system and offer various illumination options to create different atmospheres for performances. In addition to creating conditions for airy and atmospheric lighting, the organic shape also contributes to excellent acoustics. The morphology of the theater interior adeptly embeds the lighting and acoustic services while suggesting an image of floating clouds.

Envisioned as a public space, the Yiwu Grand Theater is easily accessible from all directions. Vehicular traffic can enter from the south shore, while foot bridges from the north offer pedestrians the opportunity to meander along the water and enjoy city views or the waterfront as they approach the building. An amphitheater and large open plaza extend into the water on the southern edge, while landscaped terraces offer elevated views of the site's surroundings.

The Yiwu Grand Theater is a landmark, as well as a community space for cultural activities. The complex offers different types of public space over the bridges, along the river, on the plaza, and in the valley between the two wings, all of which helps reinvigorate local cultural energy.

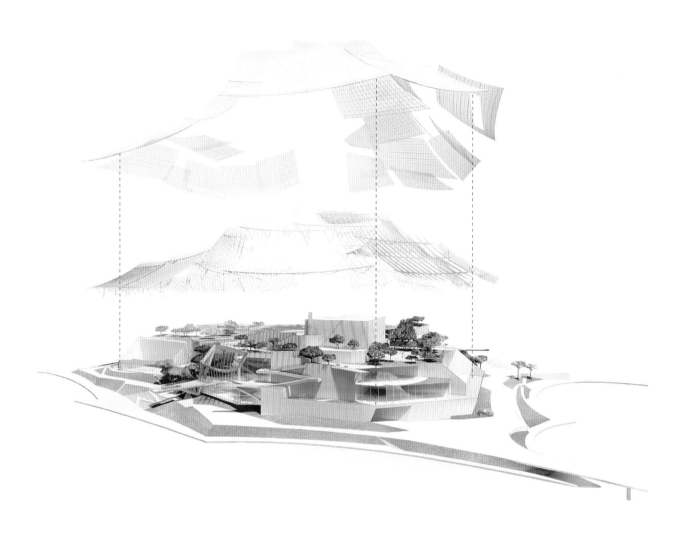

yiwu grand theater

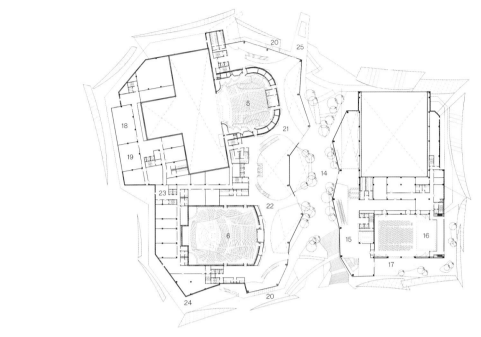

Second-Floor Plan

14. Valley Platform
15. Multi-function Hall Lobby
16. Multi-function Hall
17. Terrace
18. Dancing Rehearsal Room
19. Music Rehearsal Room
20. Visiting Route
21. Theater Balcony
22. Concert Hall Balcony
23. Back of House Lobby
24. Back of House Terrace
25. Viewing Platform

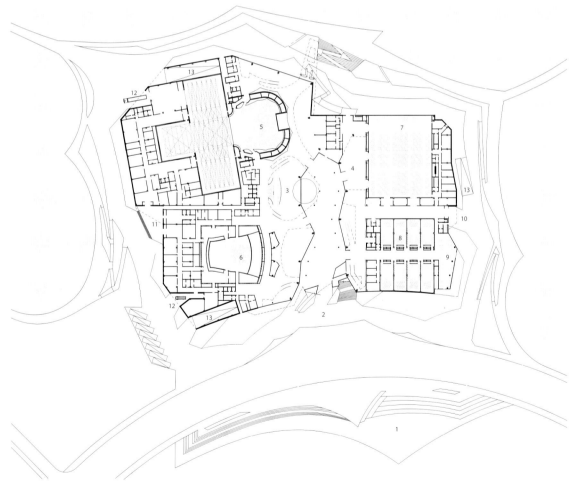

1. South Activity Plaza
2. Main Entrance
3. Theater Lobby
4. Conference Lobby
5. Grand Theater
6. Concert Hall
7. Conference Hall
8. Small Conference Hall
9. Café
10. Secondary Entrance
11. Back of House Entrance
12. Loading Dock
13. Parking Entrance

N
0 10 20   40m

Ground-Floor Plan

Founded in 2000, the China Philharmonic Orchestra gave rise to a new generation of symphonies in China. Composed of an exemplary group of musicians and conductors, it has grown into one of the most influential orchestras in the world. Located in Beijing's Central Business District, the China Philharmonic Concert Hall is the first permanent residence for the orchestra.

The concert hall is located on the south side of the Workers' Stadium, which is one of the most vibrant retail, entertainment, and nightlife areas in Beijing and is particularly popular with young people. Carving out a space of tranquility, the China Philharmonic Concert Hall is envisioned as a hidden gem and a place of peaceful respite within this bustling environment. It diversifies the local cultural scene while also creating an interesting dialogue between classical music and contemporary life.

The 26,000-square-meter (286,000-square-foot) classical music venue consists of a main concert hall and rehearsal spaces split across two floors. Surrounded by a lotus pond and greenery, the architecture is defined by a fluid and translucent facade reminiscent of a piece of jade. Inside, the soaring lobby serves as an area for mingling in soft light and provides access to the two performance halls. The transition from urban setting into a glowing and tranquil interior prepares audiences for a spiritual music journey.

china philharmonic concert hall

The grand (1,600-seat) concert hall is organized "vineyard style," with seating arranged in sloping terraces and serried rows. The white sound-reflection panels on the ceiling find their form in the lotus flower. During the day, natural light filters through the ceiling elements, while at night, visualizations will be projected onto the surface to create natural scenes that harmonize with the musical performances. The integrated experience of acoustic, floating projection, and a transition from daylight to artificial light create an immersive audiovisual experience that establishes a new paradigm for concert halls.

china philharmonic concert hall

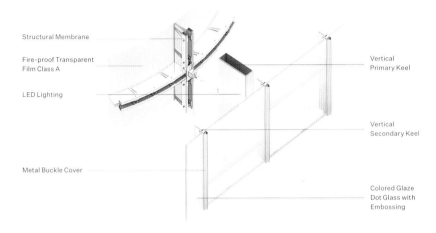

Structural Membrane

Fire-proof Transparent Film Class A

LED Lighting

Metal Buckle Cover

Vertical Primary Keel

Vertical Secondary Keel

Colored Glaze Dot Glass with Embossing

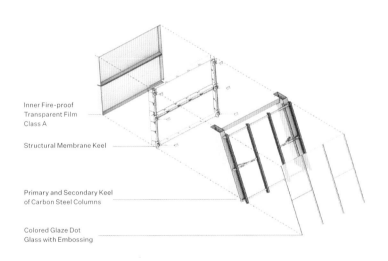

Inner Fire-proof Transparent Film Class A

Structural Membrane Keel

Primary and Secondary Keel of Carbon Steel Columns

Colored Glaze Dot Glass with Embossing

china philharmonic concert hall

On the south side of the building, a medium-sized (400-seat) rehearsal hall is nestled within curved wooden walls, whose shape optimizes the acoustic effect. The adjustable sound-reflection panels at the back of the stage can be raised to bring in natural light and views of the exterior pond. This part of the building will also contain a professional recording studio, a library, a collection gallery, offices, rehearsal rooms, and other auxiliary-function spaces.

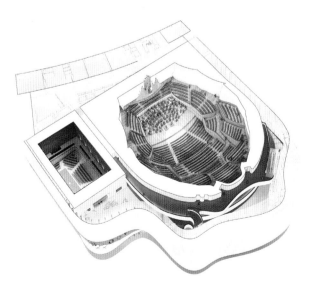

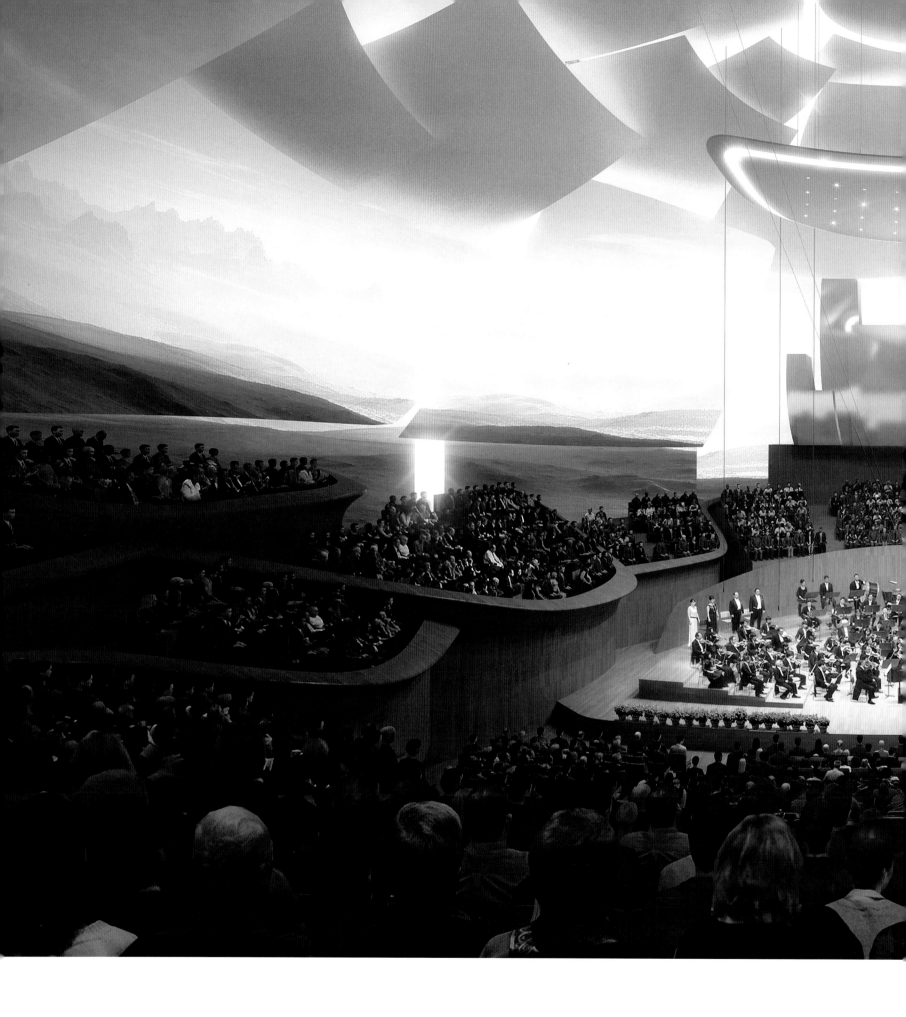

china philharmonic concert hall

Defined by its translucent facade and natural form, the China Philharmonic Concert Hall appears as a pure and sacred oasis in the middle of the city. The concert hall is also a state-of-the-art performance venue that fosters cultural exchange and stands as China's new locus for classical music.

china philharmonic concert hall

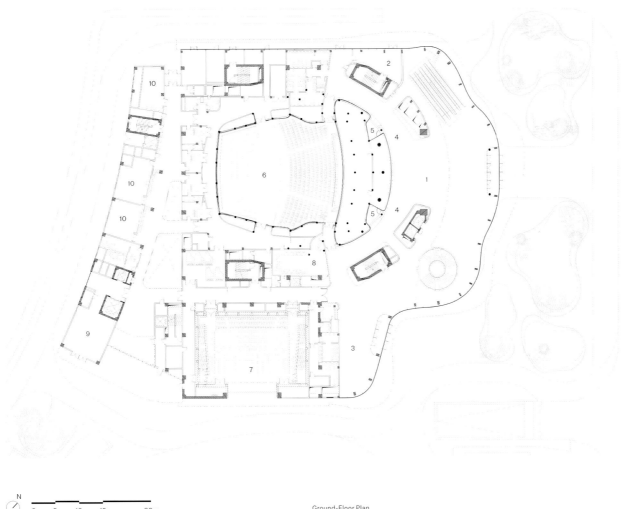

1. Lobby
2. Ticketing
3. Gift Shop
4. Gallery
5. Coat Check
6. Main Concert Hall
7. Small Concert Hall
8. VIP Room
9. Back of House Lobby
10. Makeup Room
11. Rehearsal Room

Third-Floor Plan

N

0   5   10   15   30m

Ground-Floor Plan

life

Situated on a site with a traditional *siheyuan* courtyard dating back to 1725, the YueCheng Courtyard Kindergarten embraces the existing building by softly integrating a new structure in the form of a floating roof that invigorates the historical context with an evocation of childhood freedom, love, and imagination.

The original project site, with a footprint of 9,200 square meters (99,000 square feet), consists of the eighteenth-century courtyard, an adjacent replica courtyard built in the 1990s, and a four-story modern building. The site is next to a residence for senior citizens and is surrounded by extensive green space. In shaping the project, MAD chose to remove the replica courtyard outside the authentic one while maintaining ancient trees as focal points for a new courtyard. The YueCheng Courtyard Kindergarten features a dynamic rooftop that transforms the limited space into a colorful playground.

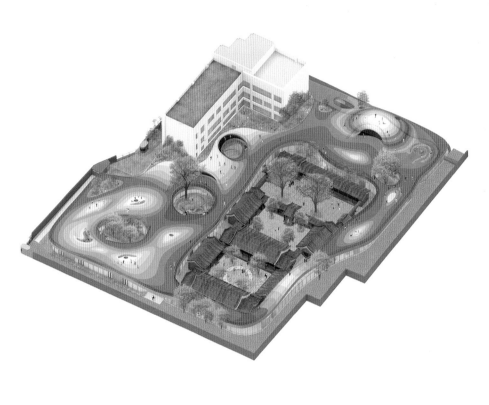

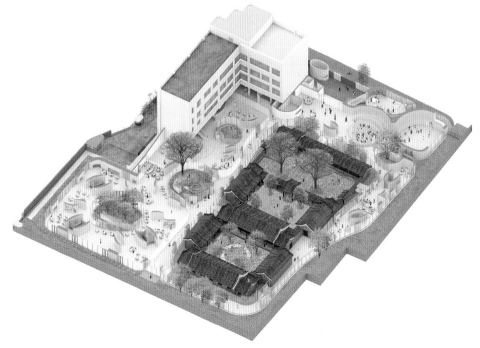

yuecheng courtyard kindergarten

yuecheng courtyard kindergarten

The kindergarten now serves as a preschool education space for 390 children from 1½ to 6 years old. Three courtyards on the ground level are designed around several ancient trees on the original site that embrace the historic building in the center. The new configuration also corresponds to the traditional *siheyuan* structure, providing learning space filled with light and air with an outdoor extension. Slides and stairs connect the courtyards to the rooftop landscape. In response to children's keen sense of scale and comfort, the interior of the building is suspended from a single aluminum grille that lowers the visual height of the scheme while instilling the interior with familial warmth. Full-height glazing allows sunlight to stream through the interior while forming a visual connection with the old courtyard house.

The transition space from the first floor to the sunken level on the east side of the lobby serves as a theater. The stage doubles as the entrance to a two-level indoor playground, which not only provides space for children's activities but also serves as an area for the whole kindergarten to participate in art and sporting events. The west side of the lobby leads to a learning area, where different mixed-age learning groups are not separated by closed walls, but instead by curved walls spaced at regular intervals—originally a supporting structure for the building. The "borderless" learning space, sprawling reading environment, and a curriculum focused on learning through play not only enrich the interaction between children but also allow teaching and learning to take place in an optimal atmosphere.

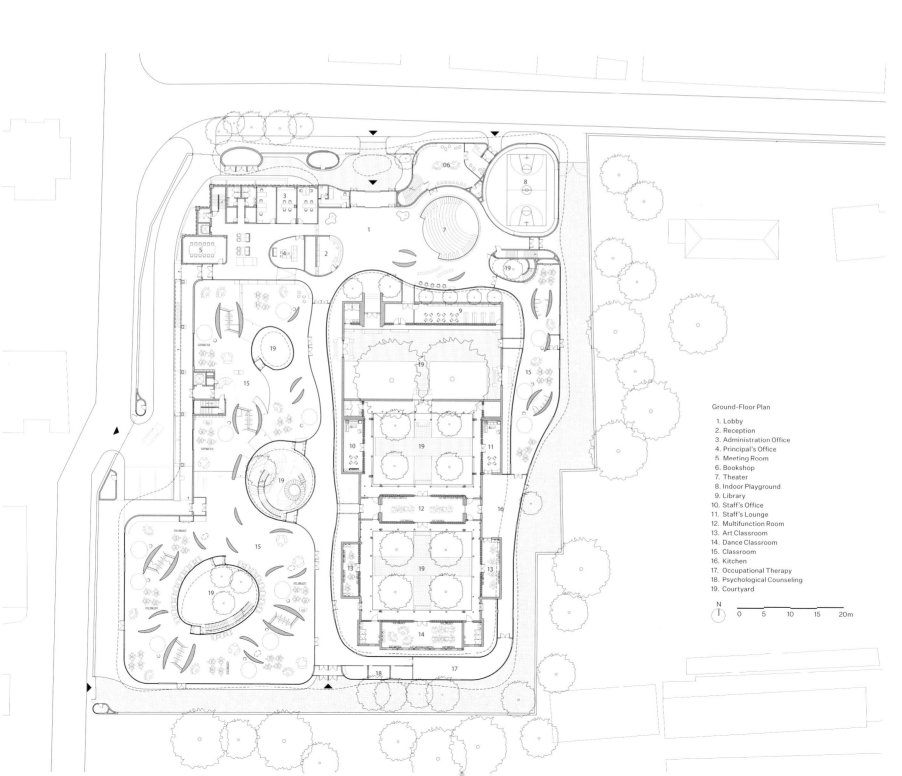

Ground-Floor Plan

1. Lobby
2. Reception
3. Administration Office
4. Principal's Office
5. Meeting Room
6. Bookshop
7. Theater
8. Indoor Playground
9. Library
10. Staff's Office
11. Staff's Lounge
12. Multifunction Room
13. Art Classroom
14. Dance Classroom
15. Classroom
16. Kitchen
17. Occupational Therapy
18. Psychological Counseling
19. Courtyard

N
0   5   10   15   20m

The YueCheng Courtyard Kindergarten contains several seemingly disparate or even contradictory parts from different historical periods, but it cultivates harmony between these elements while respecting their authenticity and individuality. Beyond this, the combination functions, as a whole, to create an open and rich experience that gives children a clear view of history while instilling in them a passion for freedom and imagination.

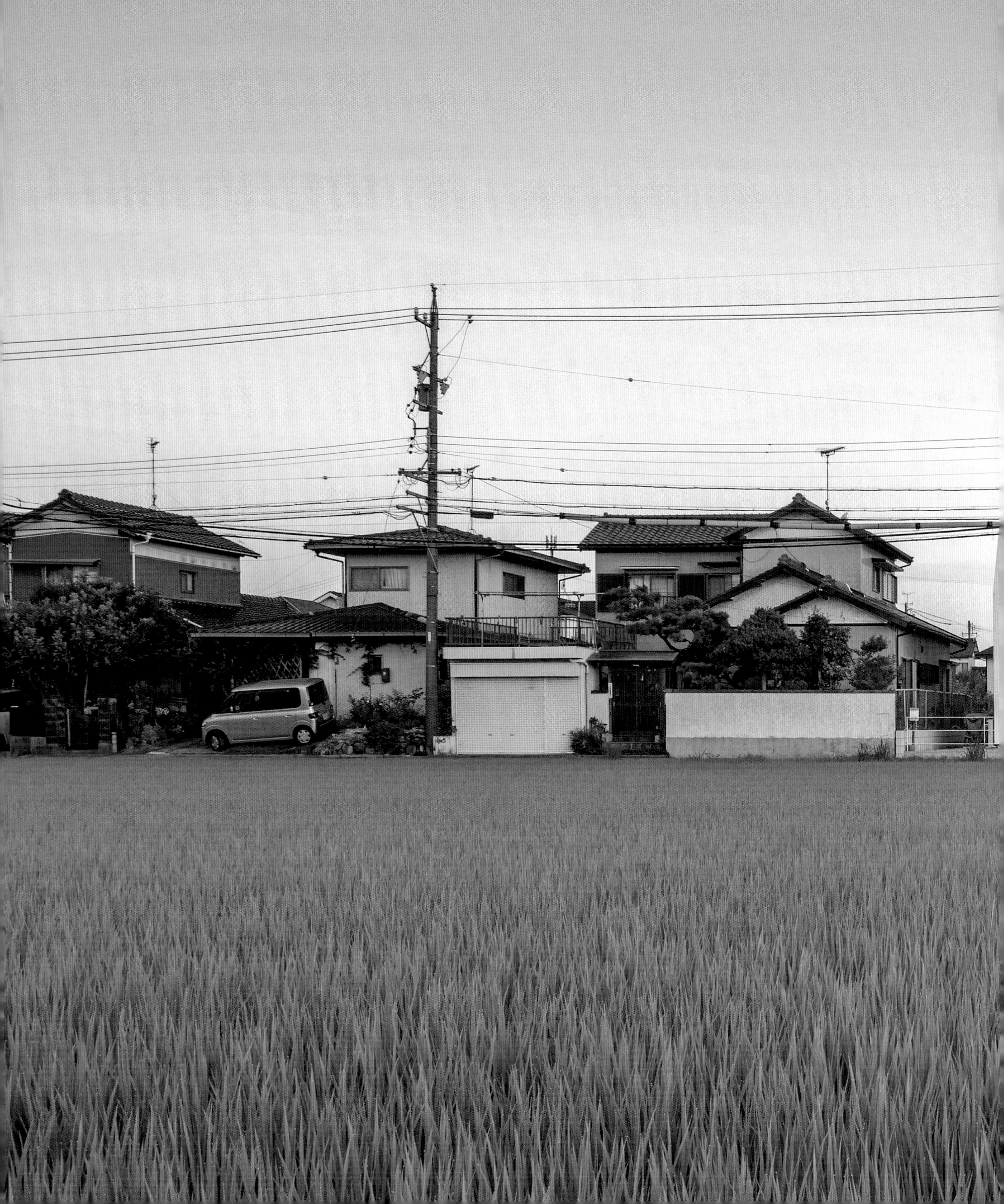

Located in the small town of Okazaki in Japan, Clover House is a kindergarten, but the project involved renovating the client's house in a way that preserved family history and allowed them to continue pursuits in education. A homelike and imaginative space for children to learn and play, Clover House also symbolizes local residents' expectations for the next generation and their vision of the future.

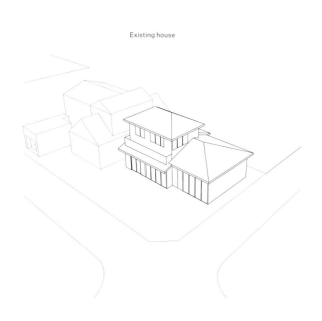

Existing house

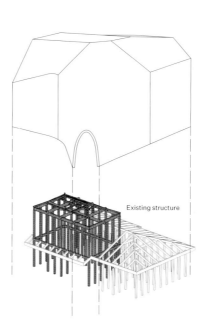

Existing structure

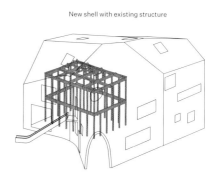

New shell with existing structure

clover house

Okazaki boasts views of rice fields and mountains, characteristic of Aichi prefecture. The kindergarten originally operated out of the client's family home, where the school began as a humble enterprise. The quarters soon became tight and did not allow for expansion of the educational space. The design goal was to create a modern educational institution where children could feel as comfortable as they do in their own homes, allowing them to grow and learn in a nurturing setting, thus both preserving the memory of a family home and fulfilling the needs of the kindergarten. The transformation started with an investigation of the existing 105-square-meter (1,130-square-foot) house. The renovation preserved the original wooden structure but added a white "otherworldly" skin that gently wraps around the building like a piece of cloth. The facade and roof utilize common soft roofing materials, such as asphalt shingles, to provide waterproofing. The envelope brings to mind a magical cave or pop-up fort that fosters curiosity and imagination.

The starting point for Clover House is the signature pitched roof. This repurposed element creates dynamic interior spaces while also integrating the history of the building and allowing for education involving the traditions and stories of Clover House. Its translucent and enclosed spaces easily adapt to different teaching activities. The windows, shaped in various geometries that are familiar to a child's eye, allow sunlight to filter through and create ever-changing shadows that trigger students' curiosity and encourage their imagination. Compared to the original assembly-line residence, the new three-dimensional wooden structure presents a much more organic and dynamic form to house the kindergarten. During the day, children and teachers can eat, study, communicate, rest, and play as if they were in a home. At night, the house reverts back to a living space for the owner's family and the schoolteachers.

clover house

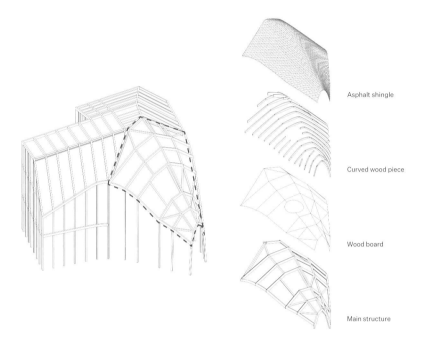

Asphalt shingle

Curved wood piece

Wood board

Main structure

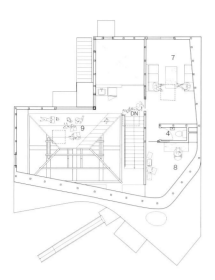

Third-Floor Plan

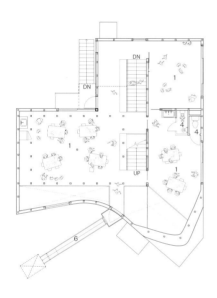

Second-Floor Plan

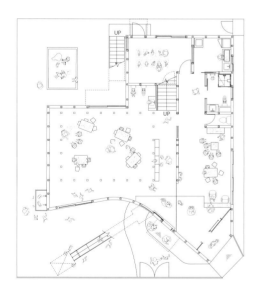

Ground-Floor Plan

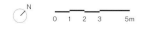

N   0 1 2 3   5m

1. Classroom   6. Slide
2. Playground   7. Living Room
3. Entrance   8. Study
4. Bathroom   9. Library
5. Kitchen

clover house

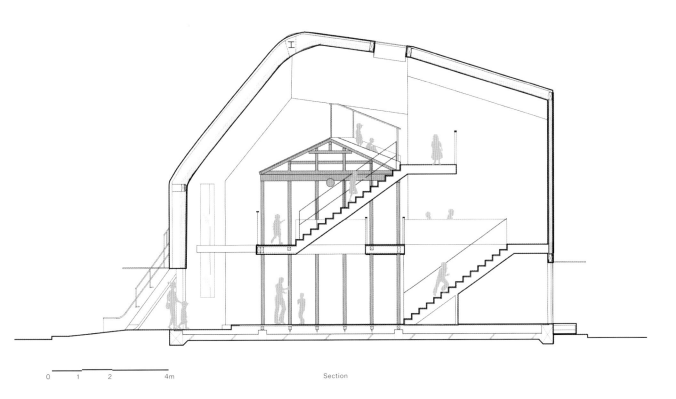

0 1 2 4m

Section

Clover House differentiates itself from traditional kindergartens by fully embracing its role as a shelter—a haven for education during the day and a home in the evening. The kindergarten's homelike environment supports Clover House's fully open teaching methodology, through which the children are encouraged to build emotional bonds and trust with each other.

Located in Jiaxing, Zhejiang province, this renovated train station rebuilds on the historic station while creating a new infrastructure annex underground. Contrary to most of the train stations in China, which tend to loom like grand palaces, this one is based on a design that integrates a borderless park into its functional arrangement, providing citizens and travelers a chance to pause and enjoy the beautiful natural environment and bringing the city center back to the people.

The train station is at the center of Jiaxing, an interconnected city in southeast China. As a key city for several major industries, Jiaxing is referred to as both the "home of silk" and the "land of agriculture and fishery." In 1921, the first Congress of the Chinese Communist Party was held in Jiaxing, marking the founding of the party. Its location bears layers of meaning, both politically and economically. Before the renovation, the station had reached its maximum capacity. In addition, the disorder of the surrounding circulation system and the lack of supporting infrastructure had led to a decline in the district.

With a footprint of 35.4 hectares (87.5 acres), the project consists of Jiaxing Train Station, two plazas, and the renovated People's Park. The design places the busy transportation junction underground, freeing the ground level of obtrusive infrastructure, and allowing the People's Park to radiate through the scheme into the city and form an urban oasis. A careful consideration of landscape and massing has formed an axis with the reconstructed old station building at its core. The reconstructed station is to be rebuilt at 1:1 scale after careful discussions with scholars and experts to restore an accurate relationship. It will become the Jiaxing Railway History Museum on completion. In contrast with the busy infrastructure beneath, the park is a place of calm.

jiaxing train station

Abundant natural light floods into the underground waiting hall through skylights and a glass curtain wall at ground level. As people move from the waiting hall to the platforms via this open and bright subterranean space, they also observe the restored old station above. In this moment, past and present meet.

The scheme also places retail functions underground, while sunken court-yards connect the underground commercial space with parkland above. A new retail area is created at the south of the station, enclosed by public lawns that can host events, festivals, concerts, or markets. A wide variety of functions and services are interconnected with each other. Visitors at street level can enter and exit the transport hub in an efficient manner, while others meander through the park, visit the railway museum, or explore the commercial area before embarking on their journeys.

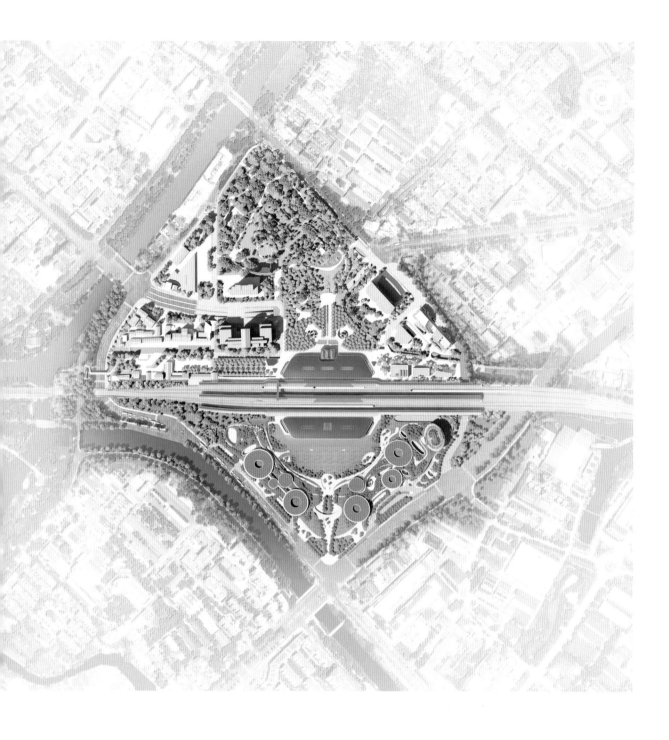

jiaxing train station

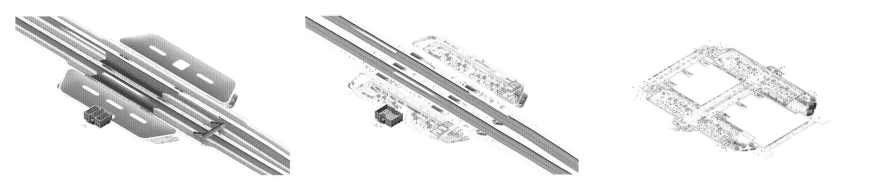

Jianxing Train Station will be completed before July 2021, which marks the 100th anniversary of the founding of the Chinese Communist Party. The scheme's emphasis on connecting with its surroundings will not only serve to increase activities and bring visitors to the area, but also enhance its retail offerings and ultimately rejuvenate the old city center.

The FENIX Museum of Migration is set within Rotterdam's historic Fenix warehouse, once the largest building of its type in the world. Commissioned by the Droom en Daad Foundation, the warehouse's renovation centers on a newly designed panoramic sightseeing platform, connecting the rich history of Rotterdam with the city's contemporary culture.

Located on the Katendrecht Peninsula, the Fenix warehouse sits within a significant immigration port in European history, and a former site of one of Europe's largest "Chinatown" districts. Throughout the past century, the Fenix warehouse has been entwined with the history of Rotterdam, most significantly when two million European emigrants departed from there to sail for America between 1880 and 1920.

To create the new museum, MAD proposes a double staircase to act as an uplifting force and a floating gesture among the historic fabric. The staircase spirals through the structure, reshaping the glass ceiling in its vortex; its winding path giving visitors the opportunity to meander and explore the museum from different perspectives. The staircase also provides access to the second-floor gallery space, where the stories of Rotterdam's history of migration are told.

To preserve the building's historical legacy, MAD's renovation embraces the structure's iconic green steel windows, as well as its concrete frame. The center of the warehouse facade is replaced by glass curtain walls that open the interior toward the outside, transforming the museum into an inviting, accessible public space for visitors. At the building's core, the large, winding staircase connects the atrium with the second floor, before continuing to the rooftop.

Breaking through the ceiling, the double spiral staircase choreographs different passages for visitors, playing with different speeds and city views. The two staircases are functionally independent from each other, while delicately touching at three moments along the spiral. In the center, an elevator passes through an opaque cylindrical shell to suddenly reveal the panoramic city view to its visitors at the top. In its entirety, the design creates a sojourn that stretches time in space to form a diverse, surreal experience.

With open sightlines toward both the river and city, the museum creates a dynamic urban corridor between the adjacent high-rise buildings. The scheme animates the waterfront district, where it provokes conversation and inspires thoughts about the history of the site, and what the future holds for the city. Reflecting on the project, Droom en Daad Foundation director Wim Pijbes commented: "The Fenix Warehouse will become a *landmark* for all those millions who left Europe from the banks of the Maas, and for everybody arriving today. It offers a great future for Rotterdam's past."

FENIX museum of migration

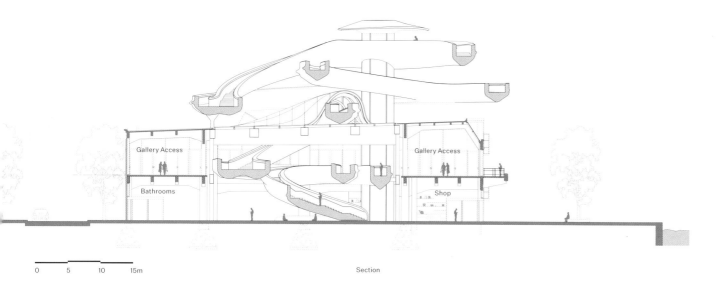

0 5 10 15m

Section

FENIX museum of migration

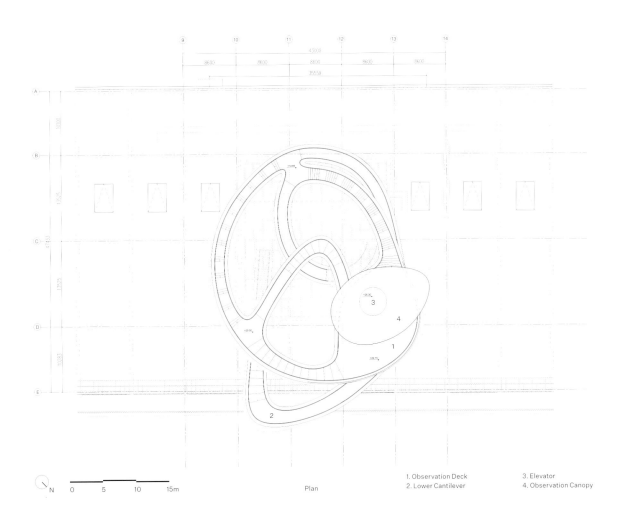

1. Observation Deck
2. Lower Cantilever
3. Elevator
4. Observation Canopy

Plan

N 0 5 10 15m

hutong bubbles

Hutong Bubble 32 / 2009 / Beijing, China
Hutong Bubble 218 / 2019 / Beijing, China

MAD's proposal for the future of Beijing was first unveiled at its exhibition *MADe IN CHINA*, shown during the 2006 Venice Architecture Biennale. Beijing 2050 imagines three scenarios for the future of the city—a green public park in Tiananmen Square, a series of floating islands above the city's Central Business District, and the "future of hutongs," which features metallic bubbles scattered throughout Beijing's oldest neighborhoods. Three years later, the first hutong bubble appeared in a small courtyard in Beijing.

Hutong Bubble 32

Hutong Bubble 32 in the Dongcheng district specifically addressed the outdated and unhygienic living conditions that led to the abandonment of the *hutongs*, unique living spaces in potentially thriving communities. The bubble includes a bathroom and a staircase that leads to the roof terrace of a newly renovated courtyard house. Its shiny exterior gives it the appearance of an alien creature, and yet at the same time, it melds into the surrounding wood, brick, and greenery. Instead of interrupting the existing urban fabric, the new complements the old.

hutong bubbles

Hutong Bubble 218

Hutong Bubble 218 is part of the Old City Renewal Research Program launched in 2014. Adjacent to several important cultural landmarks, such as the Forbidden City, the site, with a footprint of 469 square meters (5,000 square feet), was built up over hundreds of years and was converted to multifamily residency after initial use as a clinic. One sculptural bubble lands softly on the rooftop. Another connects the first and second floors with a staircase. Puncturing the roof landscape, it emerges onto the terrace and functions as an independent meeting room/shared work space that flows over the edge into the front courtyard. A mysterious aura inhabits these futuristic and surrealistic forms. Their smooth, mirrored surfaces reflect the ancient buildings, trees, and sky in the vicinity, blending into the environment.

The Hutong Bubbles function like magnets, attracting people, activities, and resources to reactivate entire neighborhoods. They are in symbiosis with the existing neighborhood. The bubbles multiply and morph to meet a community's different needs, thereby allowing local residents to continue living in these old neighborhoods.

The bubble is not regarded as a one-off. The real ambition is to see these projects as new membranes within the urban fabric by 2050, giving the traditional hutongs new life and revitalizing the communities concerned. The project intends to shift people's view away from showy new icons to focus on the everyday lives of residents.

271

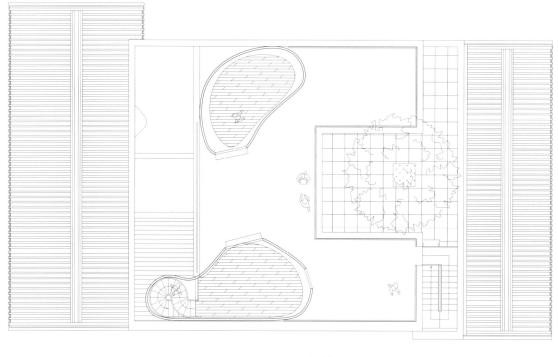

Roof Plan

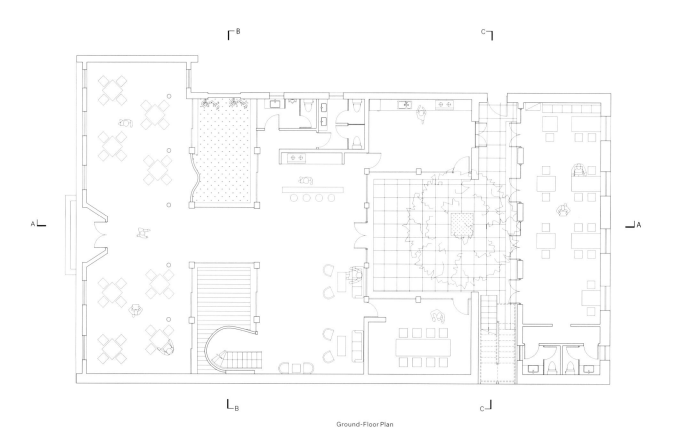

Ground-Floor Plan

N ⊕ 0 1 2   5m

hutong bubbles

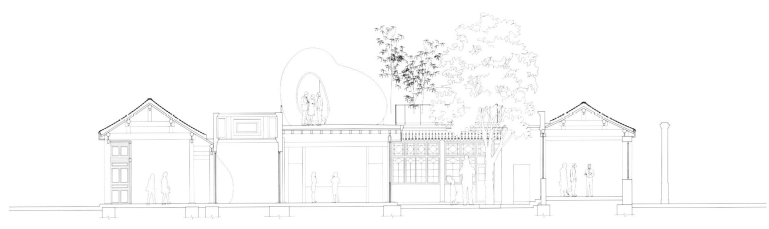

Section A-A

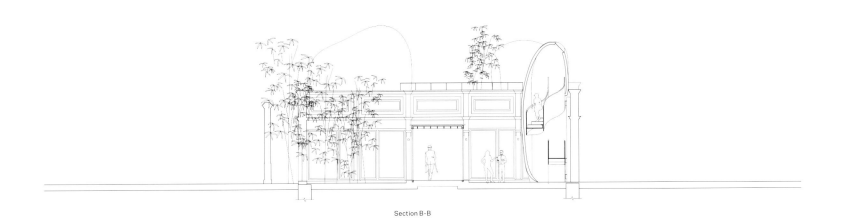

Section B-B

Section C-C

0   1   2   5m

About MAD Architects

Founded by Ma Yansong in 2004, MAD Architects is a global architecture firm committed to developing futuristic, organic, technologically advanced designs that embody a contemporary interpretation of humanity's affinity for nature. With a vision for future cities founded on the spiritual and emotional needs of residents, MAD endeavors to create a balance between humanity, the city, and the environment.

Across the world, MAD has been active in the design of urban planning schemes, complexes, museums, theaters, residential projects, and artworks—with ongoing projects in China, Italy, France, Japan, and the USA.

In addition to architecture, MAD is a pioneer in contemporary art and design. The firm has participated in major global events and exhibitions, while an array of their architectural models have recently been acquired by the well-known Center Pompidou and M+ Museum as part of their permanent collections. MAD's design advances have also been chronicled in a series of books: *Mad Dinner*, *Bright City*, *Ma Yansong*, *Shanshui City*, and *MAD X*.

MAD has offices in Beijing (China), Jiaxing (China), Los Angeles (USA), and Rome (Italy), led by three principal partners Ma Yansong, Dang Qun, and Yosuke Hayano. Seven associate partners include Liu Huiying, Andrea D'Antrassi, Lu Junliang (Dixon), Kin Li, Fu Changrui, Tiffany Dahlen, Flora Lee.

Ma Yansong
Founder & Principal Partner

Beijing-born architect Ma Yansong is recognized as an important voice in a new generation of architects. He is the first Chinese architect to win an overseas landmark project (Absolute Towers, Canada) and overseas cultural landmark project (Lucas Museum of Narrative Art, USA). As the founder of MAD Architects, Ma leads the firm's designs across various scales, with a vision of using architecture to create a new balance between society, the city, and the environment. In parallel with his design practice, he also explores the cultural value of cities and architecture on the public stage, through domestic and international solo exhibitions, publications, and artworks.

In 2008, Ma was selected as one of the "20 Most Influential Young Architects" by *ICON Magazine*, while *Fast Company* named him one of the "10 Most Creative People in Architecture in 2009" as well as one of the "100 Most Creative People in Business in 2014." In 2010, he received the "RIBA International Fellowship," while in 2014, he was named a "Young Global Leader (YGL)" by the World Economic Forum.

Ma holds a bachelor's degree from the Beijing Institute of Civil Engineering and Architecture, and holds a master's degree in Architecture from Yale University. He has served as an adjunct professor at the Beijing University of Civil Engineering and Architecture, Tsinghua University, and the University of Southern California.

Dang Qun
Principal Partner

Born in Shanghai, China, Dang Qun is a pillar of MAD's leadership. Her responsibilities include strategic development, overseeing all aspects of the firm's management around the world, and advancing MAD's company culture and values.

Dang is involved at every level of MAD's creativity and operations. She oversees all project execution, including the planning and deployment of teams. Her extensive experience in design and construction allows her to actively contribute at all project stages, from inception to completion. Dang is at the forefront of client communication and collaboration from initial concept to final product, and ensures all parties are aligned in delivering a unified design vision. She also leads MAD to actively engage and investigate cutting edge building techniques and technology, facilitating MAD's ever-growing vision and standards.

Dang holds a master's degree from Iowa State University. She has held a visiting professorship at the Pratt Institute, an assistant professorship at Iowa State University, and has received a Certificate of Merit from the American Institute of Architects.

Yosuke Hayano
Principal Partner

Yosuke Hayano was born in the Japanese region of Aichi and is a first-class registered architect in Japan. He oversees all design works at MAD, directing each design team to seamlessly materialize MAD's philosophy, from concept sketch to technical drawing to final architectural form. Yosuke also oversees MAD's design language across all scales, from the human scale to the architectural and urban scale, thus implementing MAD's unique, site-specific architectural response for each project.

Yosuke received his bachelor's degree in Materials Engineering from Waseda University in Tokyo in 2000. He gained his associate degree in Architecture from Waseda Art and Architecture School in 2001, and his master's degree in Architecture from the Architectural Association of London in 2003.

He has been the winner of several high-profile awards in his career to date, including the Architecture League of New York Young Architects Award (2006), the Design for Asia Award (2011), and the Kumamoto Artpolis Award (2011). He served as a visiting lecturer at the Waseda Art and Architecture School from 2008 to 2012, and at Tokyo University from 2010 to 2012. In addition, he served as an external examiner at the Architectural Association of London from 2015 to 2019.

MAD Architects, left to right: Ma Yansong, Dang Qun, and Yosuke Hayano

Chapter 1: Allegory

Absolute Towers

Program: Residential
Status: Completed
Location: Mississauga, Ontario, Canada
Design: 2006
Completion: 2012

Tower A: 45,000 sqm, 56 stories/height 170 m
Tower B: 40,000 sqm, 50 stories/height 150 m

Principal Architect: Ma Yansong, Yosuke Hayano,
 Dang Qun
Design Team: Yu Kui, Zhao Wei, Florian Pucher,
 Zhao Fan, Hao Yi, Yao Mengyao, Shen Jun, Robert
 Groessinger, Yi Wenzhen, Liu Yuan, Li Kunjuan,
 Max Lonnqvist, Eric Spencer

Client: Fernbrook/Cityzen
Executive Architect: BURKA Architects INC.
Structural Engineer: SIGMUND, SOUDACK &
 ASSOCIATES INC.
MEP Engineer: ECE Group
Landscape Architect: NAK Design
Interior Design: ESQAPE Design

The Cloudscape of Haikou

Program: Library, public toilet
Status: Completed
Location: Haikou, China
Design: 2019
Completion: 2021

Site Area: 4,397 sqm
Building Area: 1,380 sqm

Principal Architect: Ma Yansong, Dang Qun,
 Yosuke Hayano
Design Team: Fu Changrui, Qiang Siyang, Shang Li,
 Sun Feifei, Dayie Wu, Alan Rodríguez Carrillo, Xie
 Qilin, Beatrice Bavuso

Client: Haikou Tourism & Culture Investment Holding
 Group
Executive Architect: East China Architecture Design
 and Research Institute
Facade Consultant: RFR Shanghai
Signage Consultant: 2x4 Beijing
Interior Decorator: Beijing Ling & BuYao Interior design
Construction Contractor: Yihuida Shimizu Concrete

Shenzhen Bay Culture Park

Program: Museum
Status: Under Construction
Location: Shenzhen, China
Design: 2018
Completion: 2023

Site Area: approximately 51,000 sqm
Building Area: 181,659 sqm

Above Ground: 44,447 sqm
Below Ground: 137,212 sqm

Height:
South Venue: 31 m
North Venue: 52 m

Principal Architect: Ma Yansong, Dang Qun,
 Yosuke Hayano
Design Team: Kin Li, Tiffany Dahlen, Li Cunhao, Zhang
 Chao, Zhang Yaohui, Maria Corella, Haruka Tomoeda,
 Natawat Warotdulyavat, Yoshio Fukumori, Li Xinyun,
 Huang Jinkun, Yang Xuebiing, Tian Jin, Xu Chen,
 Lim Zi Han, Neeraj Mahajan, Li Hui, Luis Torres, Kenji
 Hada, Qiang Siyang, Gan Mengjia, Liu Hailun, Yu Lin,
 Huai Wei, Edgar S. Navarrete, Alessandro Fisalli,
 Chen Yi-en, Gong Wei, Cao Xi, Pittayapa Suriyapee,
 Lei Kaiyun

Client: Municipal Government of Shenzhen; Nanshan
 District Government of Nanshan; City of Shenzhen
 Bureau of Culture, Radio, Film, Tourism and Sports;
 City of Shenzhen; China Resources (Holdings)
 Co., Ltd.
Executive Architect: East China Architectural Design &
 Research Institute (ECADI)
Structural Engineer: Shenzhen Branch of ARUP
 Engineering Consulting (Shanghai) Co., Ltd.
MEP Consultant: IDC MEP of East China Architectural
 Design and Research Institute (ECADI)
Facade Consultant: RFR Shanghai
Landscape Design: Sasaki Associates, Shenzhen
 Metrostudio Landscape & Urban Planning Design
 Co., Ltd.
Lighting Design: Beijing Ning Field Lighting Design
 Co., Ltd.
Signage Design: Kenya Hara (Nippon Design Center,
 Inc.)
BIM Consultant: Shanghai Luban Software Limited
 Company
Traffic Consultant: PMO Static Transportation
 Consulting (Shanghai) Co., Ltd.
Traffic Evaluation: China City Development Academy
Interior Design: Shanghai Xian Dai Architectural
 Decoration & Landscape Design Research Institute
 Co., Ltd.
Acoustic Consultant: Guangdong Qiyuan Architecture
 and Construction Design Co., Ltd.
Fire Protection Consultant: Shenzhen Dingcheng
 International Construction Project Management
 Co., Ltd.

Lucas Museum of Narrative Art

Program: Museum
Status: Under Construction
Location: Los Angeles, California, USA
Design: 2015
Completion: TBA

Site Area: approximately 11 acres, 44,000 sqm

Principal Architect: Ma Yansong, Dang Qun,
 Yosuke Hayano

Design Team: Kin Li, Tiffany Dahlen, Dixon Lu, Flora Lee, Jon Kontuly, Daniel Gillen, Jordan Kanter, Daniel Weber, Zhu Yuhao, Xie Peng, Casey Kell, Carmen Carrasco, Kazushi Miyamoto, Matthew Pugh, Jacob Hu, Chris Nolop, Will Colenso, Hiroki Fujino, Ben Yuqiang, Satoko Narishige, Rozita Kahirtseva

Competition Team: Kin Li, Zhao Wei, Andrea D'Antrassi, Tiffany Dahlen, Wu Kaicong, Kek Leong Seow, Younjin Park, Daniel Weber, Cesar d Pena Del Rey, Valeria Pestereva, Wang Yiqi, Sarita Tejasmit, He Xiaokang

Client: Lucas Museum of Narrative Art
Executive Architect: Stantec
Project Management: JLL
General Contractor: Hathaway Dinwiddie Construction Company
Structural Engineer: LERA Consulting Structural Engineers
MEP/FPI: Alfa Tech
Landscape Design: Studio-MLA

Ordos Museum

Program: Museum
Status: Completed
Location: Ordos, China
Design: 2005
Completion: 2011

Site Area: 27,760 sqm
Building Area: 41,227 sqm
Height: 40 m

Principal Architect: Ma Yansong, Yosuke Hayano, Dang Qun
Design Team: Marco Zuttioni, Lin Xiaolan, Andrew C. Bryant, Howard Jiho Kim, Shang Li, Matthias Helmreich, Diego Perez, Xiang Ling, Linda Stannieder, Zheng Tao, Qin Lichao, Sun Jieming, Yin Zhao, Du Zhijian, Yuan Zhongwei, Yuan Ta, Xie Xinyu, Liu Weiwei, Felipe Escudero, Sophia Tang, Art Terry, J Travis Russett, Dustin Harris

Client: Committee Office of Ordos Government Invested Construction and Infrastructure Projects
Executive Architect: China Institute of Building Standard Design & Research
Mechanical Engineer: The Institute of Shanxi Architectural Design and Research
Facade/Cladding Consultant: SuP Ingenieure GmbH, Melendez & Dickinson Architects
Construction Contractor: Huhehaote Construction Co., Ltd
Facade Contractor: Zhuhai King Glass Engineering Co., Ltd

Xinhee Design Center

Program: Office
Status: Under Construction
Location: Xiamen, China

Design: 2010
Completion: 2022

Site Area: 15,624 sqm
Building Area: 61,534 sqm
Building Height: 45.5m

Principal Architect: Ma Yansong, Dang Qun, Yosuke Hayano
Design Team: Liu Huiying, Flora Lee, Fu Changrui, J Travis Russett, Xu Chen, Natalia Giacomino, Younjin Park, Sear Nee, Ratima Suwanrumpha, Julian Sattler, Zhang Long, Ma Ning, Wang Xiujing, Jei Kim, Zhu Jinglu, Zeng Lingyue, Jakob Beer, Liang Zhongyi, Liu Ling, Sarita Tejasmit

Client: Xinhee Co., Ltd.
Executive Architect: CCDI Group
Structural Engineer: ARUP Shenzhen
MEP Engineer: ARUP Shenzhen
Facade Consultant: RFR Shanghai
Lighting Consultant: Beijing Ning Field Lighting Design Co., Ltd.
Landscape Architect: Cicada Landscape Architecture
Interior Design: Suzhou Gold Mantis Construction Decoration, Comyang Architecture Consulting
Acoustics: SM&W

Chapter 2: Chromatic Harmony

Harbin Opera House
Program: Theater
Status: Completed
Location: Harbin, China
Design: 2010
Completion: 2015

Building Area: 79,000 sqm
Building Height: 56 m
Grand Theater Capacity: 1,600 seats
Small Theater Capacity: 400 seats

Principal Architect: Ma Yansong, Dang Qun, Yosuke Hayano
Design Team: Liu Huiying, Fu Changrui, Zhao Wei, Kin Li, Jordan Kanter, Daniel Gillen, Bas van Wylick, Zheng Fang, Julian Sattler, Jackob Beer, J Travis Russett, Sohith Perera, Colby Thomas Suter, Yu Kui, Philippe Brysse, Huang Wei, Flora Lee, Wang Wei, Xie Yibang, Lyo Hengliu, Alexander Cornelius, Alex Gornelius, Mao Beihong, Gianantonio Bongiorno, Jei Kim, Chen Yuanyu, Yu Haochen, Qin Lichao, Pil-Sun Ham, Mingyu Seol, Lin Guomin, Zhang Haixia, Li Guangchong, Wilson Wu, Ma Ning, Davide Signorato, Nick Tran, Xiang Ling, Gustavo Alfred Van Staveren, Yang Jie

Client: Harbin Songbei Investment and Development Group Co., Ltd.
Executive Architect: Beijing Institute of Architectural Design (BIAD) Institute Studio 3
Facade/Cladding Consultant: Inhabit Group, China Jingye Engineering Co., Ltd.

Facade BIM: Gehry Technologies Co., Ltd.
Landscape Architect: Beijing Turenscape Institute
Interior Design: MAD Architects, Shenzhen Keyuan Construction Group Co., Ltd.
Interior Decoration Consultant: Harbin Weimeiyuan Decoration Design Co., Ltd.
Acoustics Consultant: Acoustic and Theater Special Design & Research Studio of East China Architectural Design & Research Institute (ECADI)
Lighting Architect: China International Engineering Design & Consult Co., Ltd.
Stage Lighting and Acoustics Design: Acoustic and Theater Special Design & Research Studio of East China Architectural Design & Research Institute (ECADI)
Stage Mechanical Engineer: Beijing New Era Architectural Design Ltd.
Signage Design: Shenzhen Freesigns Signage Co., Ltd.

Chaoyang Park Plaza

Program: Office, commercial, residential
Status: Completed
Location: Beijing, China
Design: 2012
Completion: 2017

Site Area: 30,763 sqm
Building Area: 223,009 sqm
Above Ground: 128,177 sqm
Below Ground: 94,832 sqm
Building Height: 142 m

Principal Architect: Ma Yansong, Dang Qun, Yosuke Hayano
Design Team: Kin Li, Liu Huiying, Fu Changrui, Zhao Wei, Li Guangchong, Lin Guomin, Bennet Hu Po-Kang, Nathan Kiatkulpiboone, Yang Jie, Julian Sattler, Younjin Park, Zhu Jinglu, Xue Yan, Zheng Fang, Matteo Vergano, Wing Lung Peng, Gustavo Maya, Li Yunlong, Tiffany Dahlen, Gustavo Alfred Van Staveren

Client: Smart-hero (HK) Investment Development Limited
Executive Architect: CCDI Group
Facade Consultant: RFR Asia
Facade Optimization: RFR Asia, Sane Form Limited
Interior Design (Office and Commercial): MADA s.p.a.m., Supercloud Studio
Interior Design (Residential): ARMANI/CASA Interior Design Studio
Signage Design: Kenya Hara (Nippon Design Center, Inc.)
Landscape Architect: Greentown Akin Landscape Architecture Co., Ltd.
Interior Lighting Consultant: M&W Lighting Limited
Landscape Lighting Consultant: Beijing Junhao Lighting Design Co., Ltd.
LEED Certification Consultant: Shenzhen Institute of Building Research Co., Ltd.

Nanjing Zendai Himalayas Center

Program: Office, commercial, residential, hotel
Status: Completed
Location: Nanjing, China
Design: 2012
Completion: 2020

Site Area: 93,597 sqm
Building Area: 628,835 sqm
Above Ground: 383,264 sqm
Below Ground: 245,571 sqm
Height: 120 m

Principal Architect: Ma Yansong, Dang Qun, Yosuke Hayano
Design Team: Kin Li, Liu Huiying, Fu Changrui, Wu Kaicong, Tiffany Dahlen, Andrea D'Antrassi, Fu Xiaoyi, Shang Li, Zhu Jinglu, Zhang Lu, Xue Yan, Tong Junfeng, Benjamin Scott Lepley, Wang Tao, Achille Tortini, Kang Mu-jung, Zhang Xiaomei, Chen Siyu, Yao Cong, Shu Sai, Seow Kek Leong, William Lewis, Liang Zhongyi, Zheng Chengwen, Huang Yanyan, Zeng Hao, Nathan Kiatkulpiboone, Tristan Brasseur

Client: Jiangsu Zendai Commercial & Cultural Development Co., Ltd.
Executive Architect: CCDI Group, Kingdom Architecture Design, Boyi Design
Facade Consultant: Konstruct West Partners
Landscape Architect: Earth Asia Design Group (EADG)
BMI: CCDI Group
Interior Design (Hotel): Steve Leung Designers
Interior Design (Commercial): Woods Bagot Shanghai
Lighting Design: LEOX Design Partnership
Signage Design: Beijing Shiyu Four-Dimension Wayfinding System Planning & Designing
Traffic Consultant: Sinclair Knight Merz (Shanghai) Co., Ltd., Nanjing Municipal Design and Research Institute

Gardenhouse

Program: Residential, commercial
Status: Completed
Location: Beverly Hills, California, USA
Design: 2013
Completion: 2020

Site Area: 2,400 sqm
Building Area: 4,460 sqm
Height: 18 m

Principal Architect: Ma Yansong, Dang Qun, Yosuke Hayano
Design Team: Flora Lee, Dixon Lu, Li Guangchong, Jon Kontuly, Joanna Tan, Chris Hung-Yu Chen, Wenshan Xie, Cesar d Pena Del Rey, Jeffrey Miner

Client: PALISADES
Executive Architect: Gruen Associates
General Contractor: DHC Builders, Inc.
Structural Engineer: John Labib + Associates (JLA)

MEP Engineer: Breen Engineering, Inc.
Landscape Architect: Gruen Associates
Green Wall Specialist: Seasons Landscaping
Interior Design: Rottet Studio
Civil Engineering: Kimley-Horn

UNIC

Program: Residential
Status: Completed
Location: Paris, France
Design: 2012
Completion: 2020

Site Area: 1,033 sqm
Building Area: 6,600 sqm
Height: 50 m

Principal Architect: Ma Yansong, Dang Qun, Yosuke Hayano
Design Team: Andrea d'Antrassi, Flora Lee, Zhao Wei, Wu Kaicong, Daniel Gillen, Jiang Bin, Tristan Brasseur, Juan Valeros, Gustavo Alfred Van Staveren, Xin Dogterom, Juan Pablo, Cesar d Pena Del Rey, Natalia Giacomino, Torsten Radunski, Rozita Kahirtseva

Client: Emerige
Executive Architect: BIECHER
Structural Engineer: BECIP–BET Structure
MEP Engineer: ESPACE TEMPS–BET Fluides
Landscape Architect: PHYTOLAB –BET Paysagiste
Interior Design: Charles Zana
Project Management: Artelia
Constructor: Vinci Sicra Île-de-France

Jiaxing Civic Center

Program: Museum, civic center
Status: Under Construction
Location: Jiaxing, China
Design: 2019
Completion: 2023

Site Area: 126,740 sqm
Building Area: approximately 180,000 sqm
Above Ground 72,351 sqm
Below Ground 107,950 sqm
Height: 38 m

Principal Architect: Ma Yansong, Dang Qun, Yosuke Hayano
Design Team: Kin Li, Fu Changrui, Liu Huiying, Yin Jianfeng, Alessandro Fisalli, Fu Xiaoyi, Chen-Hsiang Chao, He Yiming, Thoufeeq Ahmed, Chen Hao, He Xiaowen, Zhang Yaohui, Guo Xuan, Edgar Navarrete, Claudia Hertrich, Deng Wei, Zhang Xiaomei, Chen Nianhai, Li Cunhao, Sun Feifei, Punnin Sukkasem, Manchi Yeung, Li Yingzhou

Client: Jiaxing Highway Investment Co., Ltd.
Executive Architects: East China Architectural Design & Research Institute, Shanghai Municipal Engineering Design Institute (Group) Co., Ltd.
Facade consultant: RFR Shanghai

Landscape Consultant: Earthasia Design Group, Yong-High Landscape Design Consulting Co.Ltd
Interior Design consultant: Shanghai Xian Dai Architectural Decoration & Landscape Design Research Institute CO., Ltd
Signage Consultant: Nippon Design Center, Inc.
Lighting Consultant: Beijing Sign Lighting Industry Group
Traffic Consultant: Shanghai Municipal Engineering Design Institute (Group) Co., Ltd.

Chapter 3: Elemental Landscape

Tunnel of Light

Program: Renovation, Land Art
Status: Completed
Location: Echigo-Tsumari, Japan; 2018 Echigo Tsumari Art Festival
Design: 2016
Completion: 2018

Principal Architect: Ma Yansong, Yosuke Hayano, Dang Qun
Design Team: Hiroki Fujino, Kazushi Miyamoto, Yuki Ishigami

Executive Architect: Green Sigma

Yabuli Entrepreneurs' Congress Center

Program: Conference Center
Status: Completed
Location: Yabuli, China
Design: 2017
Completion: 2021

Site Area: 22,000 sqm
Building Area: 16,198 sqm
Height: 23.3 m

Principal Architect: Ma Yansong, Dang Qun, Yosuke Hayano
Design Team: Liu Huiying, Tiffany Dahlen, Li Guangchong, Deng Wei, Sun Shouquan, Fu Xiaoyi, Huai Wei, Song Chi, Zhao Meng, Wang Shuobin, Tian Jin

Client: China Entrepreneur Forum
Executive Architect: China Architecture Design & Research Group
Facade Consultant: Kighton Facade Consultant, RFR Shanghai
Landscape Architect: BJF International Design
Interior Design: Shanghai Xian Dai Architectural Decoration & Landscape Design Research Institute Co., Ltd.
Lighting Design: Brandston Partnership Inc.
Signage Design: Dongdao Creative Branding Group

Quzhou Sports Park

Program: Sports stadium, gymnasium, natatorium, training center

Status: Under Construction
Location: Quzhou, China
Design: 2018
Completion: 2022

Site Area: 574,931 sqm
Building area: 390,074 sqm
30,000-capacity Stadium: 58,565 sqm/Height 45 m
10,000-capacity Gymnasium: 70,223 sqm/Height 44 m
Natatorium: 32,505 sqm/Height 44 m
Training Center: 13,310 sqm/Height 21 m

Principal Architect: Ma Yansong, Dang Qun,
    Yosuke Hayano
Design Team: Liu Huiying, Kin Li, Fu Changrui, Xu Chen,
    Iting Lien, Li Gang, Li Cunhao, Kyung Eun Na, Ma Yin,
    Thoufeeq Ahmed, Tian Jin, Zhou Haimeng, Li Hui,
    Xiao Yuha, Ma Yue, Alessandro Fisalli, Luis Torres,
    Zhang Kai, Melanie Weitz, Yuki Ishigami, Song
    Minzhe, Su Le, Pittayapa Suriyapee, Kang Wenzhao,
    Connor Hymes, Neeraj Mahajan, Zhang Bo, Yu Lin, Li
    Guangchong, Hwiyeong Jeong, Chen Shijie, Zhang
    Yufei, Cao Xi, Wang Qi, Liu Hailun, Li Yingzhou,
    Zheng Kangcheng, Cievanard Nattabowonphal,
    Zhang Xiaomei

Client: Quzhou West District Development and
    Construction Management Committee Class A,
    Quzhou Baoye Sports Construction & Operation
    Co., Ltd.
Executive Architect: CCDI Group
Landscape Architect: PWP Landscape Architecture,
    Earthasia Design Group (EADG), Young-High
    Landscape Design
Structural Engineer: Schlaich Bergermann Partner
    (SBP), Structure Center of CCDI
Mechanical and Electrical Consultant: SC Consultant
    Limited
Facade Consultant: RFR Shanghai, Huge Span Design
    (Shanghai) Co., Ltd.
Lighting Consultant: Beijing United Artists Lighting
    Design
Signage Design: Kenya Hara (Nippon Design Center,
    Inc.)
Interior Design Drawings Development: CCDI Group,
    Shanghai Xian Dai Architectural Decoration &
    Landscape Design Research Institute Co., Ltd.
Constructor: Shanghai Baoye Group

Huangshan Mountain Village

Program: Residential
Status: Completed
Location: Huangshan, China
Design: 2009
Completion: 2016

Huangshan Taiping Lake Master Plan
Site Area: 1,186,520 sqm

Huangshan Mountain Village (Phase One)
Site Area: 189,882 sqm
Building Area: 69,586 sqm

Principal Architect: Ma Yansong, Dang Qun,
    Yosuke Hayano
Design Team: Liu Huiying, Philippe Brysse, Zhao Wei,
    Tiffany Masako Dahlen, Luke Lu, Wang Deyuan,
    Jakob Beer, Li Guangchong, Kayla Lee, Geraldine Lo,
    Alejandra Obregon, Zeng Lingdong, Achille Tortini,
    Matthew Rosen, Gustavo Maya, Zheng Fang, Sarita
    Tejasmit, Augustus Chan, Jeong-Eun Lee

Client: Greenland Hong Kong Holdings Limited
Executive Architect: HS Architects
Interior Design: Suzhou Gold Mantis Construction
    Decoration
Landscape Architect: Broadacre Source Landscape
Facade Architect: Xi'an Aircraft Industrial Decoration
    Engineering Co., Ltd.
Lighting Design: Shanghai Mofo Lighting

Yiwu Grand Theater

Program: Theater
Status: Under Construction
Location: Yiwu, China
Design: 2018
Completion: 2023

Project Area:
Site Area: 47,000 sqm
Building Area: 107,050 sqm
Height: 43.6 m
Grand Theater: 1,600 seats
Concert Hall: 1,200 seats
International Conference Center: 2,000-person capacity
Multifunctional Hall: 500 seats

Principal Architect: Ma Yansong, Dang Qun,
    Yosuke Hayano
Design Team: Liu Huiying, Zhu Yuhao, I-ting Lien,
    Zheng Chengwen, Fu Xiaoyi, Jordan Demer, Zhang
    Long, Lu Zihao, Wang Shuang, Connor Hymes,
    Maria Soledad, Zhang Kai, Otrebor Jean-Francois,
    Hwiyeong Jeong, Xiao Yuhan, Wang Shuobin,
    Jing-Chang Hu, Yu-Fu Huang, Huang Jinkun,
    Wu Qiaoling, Melanie Weitz, Zhou Rui, Deng Wei

Client: Administration Committee of Silk Road New
    District of Yiwu
Culture, Broadcasting & Television, Tourism and Sports
    Bureau of Yiwu
Yiwu City Construction Investment Group Limited
Executive Architect: East China Architectural Design &
    Research Institute
Acoustics: Acoustic & Theater Research Studio
    of ECADI
Facade Consultant: RFR Shanghai
Landscape Architect: Earthasia Design Group (EADG)
Interior Design: Shanghai Xian Dai Architectural
    Decoration & Landscape Design Research Institute
    Co., Ltd.
Lighting Design: Beijing Ning Field Lighting Design
    Co., Ltd.
Signage Design: Kenya Hara (Nippon Design
    Center, Inc.)

Theater Equipment: Kunkel Consulting
Theater Management: Poly Theater Design
    and Construction

China Philharmonic Concert Hall

Program: Music hall
Status: Under Construction
Location: Beijing, China
Design: 2014
Completion: 2022

Site: 11,600 sqm
Building Area: 26,587 sqm
Building Height: 24 m
Main Concert Hall Capacity: 1,600 seats
Small Concert Hall Capacity: 350 seats

Principal Architect: Ma Yansong, Dang Qun,
    Yosuke Hayano
Design Team: Kin Li, Liu Huiying, Zeng Hao, Zhao Wei,
    Xiao Ying, Fu Xiaoyi, Wang Qi, Wang Shuobin, Zheng
    Chengwen, Jing-Chang Hu, He Xiaokang, Jacob Hu,
    Brecht Van Acker, Wang Deyuan, Shen Chen, Dora
    Lam, Ben Yuqiang

Client: China Philharmonic Orchestra
Executive Architect: Radio, Film & TV Design and
    Research Institute (DRFT)
Acoustics: Nagata Acoustics; Radio, Film & TV Design
    and Research Institute (DRFT)
Structural Engineer: CCDI Group
Facade Consultant: RFR Shanghai
Interior Design: MAD Architects, Beijing Honggao
    Architectural Decoration and Construction Design
    Co., Ltd.
Lighting Consultant: SIGN Lighting
Stage Lighting and Acoustics Design: Radio, Film & TV
    Design and Research Institute (DRFT)
Landscape Architect: Palm Design Co., Ltd.
Signage Design: Zheng Bang Creative (Beijing) Brand
    Technology Company Limited
Planning of Traffic Facilities: Beijing Homedale Institute
    of Urban Planning & Architectural Design

Chapter 4: Life

Yuecheng Courtyard Kindergarten

Program: Kindergarten
Status: Completed
Location: Beijing, China
Design: 2017
Completion: 2020

Site Area: 9,275 sqm
Building Area: 10,778 sqm
Height: 21.05 m

Principal Architect: Ma Yansong, Dang Qun,
    Yosuke Hayano
Design Team: He Wei, Fu Changrui, Xiao Ying,
    Fu Xiaoyi, Chen Hungpin, Yin Jianfeng, Zhao Meng,
    Yang Xuebing, Kazushi Miyamoto, Dmitry Seregin,

Zhang Long, Ben Yuqiang, Cao Xi, Ma Yue,
Hiroki Fujino

Client: Yuecheng Group
Executive Architect: China Academy of Building
    Research
Interior Design: MAD Architects, Supercloud Studio
Landscape Architect: MAD Architects, ECOLAND
    Planning and Design Corporation

Clover House

Program: Kindergarten
Status: Completed
Location: Okazaki, Japan
Design: 2012
Completion: 2016

Site Area: 283 sqm
Building Area: 134 sqm
Total Floor Area: 300 sqm

Principal Architect: Ma Yansong, Yosuke Hayano,
    Dang Qun
Design Team: Takahiro Yonezu, Yukan Yanagawa,
    Hiroki Fujino, Julian Sattler, Davide Signorato,
    Yuki Ishigami

Client: Kentaro Nara/Tamaki Nara
Constructor: Kira Construction Inc.
Structural Engineer: Takuo Nagai

Jiaxing Train Station

Program: Transportation Infrastructure, commercial
Status: Under Construction
Location: Jiaxing, China
Design: 2019
Completion: 2021

Site Area: 354,000 sqm
Building Area: approximately 280,000 sqm

Principal Architect: Ma Yansong, Dang Qun,
    Yosuke Hayano
Design Team: Liu Huiying, Cao Chen, Reinier Simons,
    Yao Ran, Fu Xiaoyi, Yu Lin, Chen Wei, He Shunpeng,
    Cheng Xiangju, Kaushik Raghuraman, Chen Nianhai,
    Deng Wei, Cao Xi, Sun Mingze, Huang Zhiyu, Zhang
    Kai, Li Zhengdong, Dayie Wu, Huai Wei, Claudia
    Hertrich, Liu Zifan, Xie Qilin, Alan Rodríguez Carrillo,
    Qiang Siyang, Hou Jinghui, Li Xinyun, Yin Jianfeng,
    Mathias Juul Frost, Lei Lei, Lu Zihao

Client: Jiaxing Modernservice Industry Development &
    Investment (Group) Co., Ltd.
Executive Architects: Tongji Architectural Design
    (Group) Co., Ltd., China Railway Siyuan Survey and
    Design Group Co., Ltd.
Structural Consultant: LERA Consulting Structural
    Engineers
Facade Consultant: RFR Shanghai
Landscape Consultant: Z'scape Landscape Planning
    and Design

Lighting Consultant: Beijing Sign Lighting Industry Group
Signage Consultant: NDC CHINA, Inc.
Heritage Consultant: Shanghai Shuishi Architectural
    Design & Planning Corp., Ltd.
Interior Design Consultant: Shanghai Xian Dai
    Architectural Decoration & Landscape Design
    Research Institute Co., Ltd.

FENIX Museum of Migration

Program: Museum
Status: Under Construction
Location: Rotterdam, Netherlands
Design: 2018
Completion: 2025

Site Area: 13,200 sqm
Building Area: 13,200 sqm
Ramp Area: 1,050 sqm
Height: 28.3 m

Principal Architect: Ma Yansong, Dang Qun,
    Yosuke Hayano
Design Team: Andrea D'Antrassi, Marco Gastoldi,
    Neeraj Mahajan, Edgar Navarrete, Cievanard
    Nattabowonphal, Jordan Demer, Alessandro Fisalli,
    Chen Yien, Claudia Hertrich, Pittayapa Suriyapee

Client: Droom en Daad Foundation

Monumental Architecture Renovation: Bureau
    Polderman
Construction Advisor: IMd Raadgevende Ingenieurs
Steel Constructor: CSM Steelstructures
Cladding Constructor: Central Industry Group (CIG)
Lighting Consultant: Beersnielsen lichtontwerpers
Installation Design: Bosman Bedrijven
Installation Advisor: DWA
Building Physics Advisor: LBP Sight

Hutong Bubbles

Hutong Bubble 32
Program: Renovation
Status: Completed
Location: Beijing, China
Design: 2008
Completion: 2009

Site Area: 140 sqm
Building Area: 10 sqm

Principal Architect: Ma Yansong, Dang Qun
Design Team: Dai Pu, Yu Kui, Stefanie Helga Paul, He
    Wei, Shen Jianghai
Construction Engineer: Beijing Nade Environmental Art
    Design Co., Ltd.

Hutong Bubble 218
Program: Renovation
Status: Completed
Location: Beijing, China
Design: 2015
Completion: 2019

Site Area: 469 sqm
Building Area: 305.1 sqm

Principal Architect: Ma Yansong, Dang Qun,
    Yosuke Hayano
Design Team: He Wei, Li Yuanhao, Shang Li, Fu
    Changrui, Wang Tao, Dmitry Seregin, Cesar D. Rey
Executive Architect: Beijing Architectural Design and
    Research Institute EA4
Constructor: First Construction Engineering Office
    of Beijing Dalong Construction Group Co., Ltd.

Image Credits

Adam Mørk: 82–83, 84 (top), 90 (left), 91, 92–93, 96 (both), 97, 139, 140–41, 143, 144

Aogvision: 28 (left), 32, 34 (both), 35 (both), 165, 166–67, 172 (both), 173, 178 (bottom), 185 (both), 186–87, 253 (bottom right), 256–56

ArchExist: 3, 10 right, 29 right, 33, 35 right, 104–5, 106 (both), 108 (both), 109 (top left), 142 (both), 168 (both), 169 (left), 170, 171, 224–25, 226, 228 (both), 229, 233 (bottom)

CreatAR Images: 27, 28 right, 29 left, 30, 31, 34, 35 left, 54–55, 67, 68–69, 70, 72–73, 74 (both), 75, 78–79, 114–15, 116 (right), 122, 169 (right)

Dan Honda: 242 (both), 243 (both)

Daniele Dainelli: 265

Darren Bradley: 126 (bottom), 127 (right), 134 (top and bottom right)

DBOX: 52

Iwan Baan: 9, 19, 20, 21, 22 (middle and right), 23 (right), 61, 62–63, 64 (left), 65 (all), 86–87, 95

Olafur Eliasson: 293

Fancyimages | WangKan: 119

Fang Zhenning: 64 (right), 290

Fernando Guerra: 189, 193 (bottom right)

Fuji Koji: 236, 237 (bottom), 238–39, 240, 241 (both)

Greg Mei: 279

Hufton+Crow: 84 (bottom), 85, 88–89, 90 (right), 94 (both), 101, 103, 107 (both), 109 (bottom), 197 (left), 230 (both), 231 (both)

Hunter Kerhart: 58–59

Jared Chulski: 145

Laurian Ghinitoiu: 190–91, 192 (right), 193 (left and top right), 194–95, 197 (right)

Ma Yansong: 156–57, 160 (bottom), 163 (top)

MAD Architects: 42–43, 118, 133, 174 (bottom), 237 (top), 244 (left), 262 (bottom), 291

Manolo Langis: 132

Mike Kelley: 124–25

Mir: 51, 53, 56–57, 259, 260, 261

Nacasa & Partners, Inc.: 160 (left, top right), 161 (all), 162

Nic Lehoux: 126 (top), 127 (left), 128–29, 130–31, 134 (left), 135 (both)

Rasmus Taun: 234–35

Shu He: 192 (left), 266 (all)

Tian Fangfang: 109 (right), 233 (top), 267, 268–69, 270 (both), 271 (both), 272–73, 276–77

Tokamachi Tourist Association: 158 (bottom)

Tom Arban: 22 (left), 23 (left)

Xia Zhi: 9 (top), 10 (bottom), 110–11, 117, 123 (both)

285

MAD rhapsody

First published in the United States of America
in 2021 by
Rizzoli Electa
A division of Rizzoli International Publications, Inc.
300 Park Avenue South
New York, NY 10010
www.rizzoliusa.com

For Rizzoli Electa:
Charles Miers, Publisher
Margaret Rennolds Chace, Associate Publisher
Ellen R. Cohen, Senior Editor
Kaija Markoe, Production Manager
Lynn Scrabis, Managing Editor
Natalie Danford, Copyeditor

For MAD Team:
Wang Mengyao, Fiona Qi Ziying, Angel Lim Zi Qi,
Cai Yixuan, Tammy Xiaozhang Xie, Shao Yixue,
Edgar S. Navarrete

Design: Office of Luke Bulman

2021 2022 2023 2024 2025 / 10 9 8 7 6 5 4 3 2 1

ISBN: 978-0-8478-6962-6
Library of Congress Control Number: 2021937395

Printed in Hong Kong

Rebuilt WTC
2001 / New York, New York, USA / Urban Concept

In 2001, the September 11 attacks wielded unforgettable
impact on New York City, and plans were made for the
former site of the World Trade Center to be rebuilt as
a memorial to those lost in the historic event. Envisioned
by Ma Yansong, Rebuilt WTC is a programmed landscape flowing above the site: a horizontal urban landscape
joining the surrounding buildings and reclaiming a public
arena in the heart of the city. This new organizational
structure diminishes the machine aesthetic and social
divisions of the modern era. The greatest monument we
can offer is renewed public space and an architecture
of cohesion.

Tiananmen People's Park
The proposal transforms Tiananmen Square into a forest. The massive plaza is stripped of its political and transportation functions. It is instead an urban space filled with life and green at the heart of Beijing.

Beijing 2050
2006 / Beijing, China / Urban Intervention

After witnessing the way China's rapid development was eroding Beijing's delicate urban fabric, MAD proposed Beijing 2050 at the 2006 Venice Architecture Biennale. Beijing 2050 imagines three scenarios for the future ambitions of Beijing.

Hutong Bubbles
MAD conceives a network of metallic bubbles to be developed in Beijing's historic neighborhoods. Inserted into the city's existing urban fabric, they are envisioned as attracting new people, activities, and resources to these aging and neglected communities.

Floating Island
MAD creates a floating island over the Central Business District in Beijing for a postmodern society. The future of Beijing will be interrelated architecture rather than a sea of individual glass boxes. Spaces with different functions will be elevated above the existing business district, hatching new horizontal connectivity.

Fish Tank
2004 / New York, New York, USA / Winner of the 2006
Architectural League Prize for Young Architects
Size: 300 (L) × 300 (W) × 400 (H) mm [11.8 (L) ×
11.8 (W) × 15.75 (H) inches]

We are seeking
living space for fish in the city,
and the conditions of human beings and fish
have to be inverted:
the fish should dominate.
The space begins to split.
Cubic boxes have melted down.
The collapse of low-quality cubic space
marks the end of the machine era.

Contradiction with square boxes
does not signify we are against mainstream culture.
Civilians own the ideal of mainstream culture.
They deserve more attention
and independence.

Ink Ice
2006 / Beijing, China / Installation
Materials: Water, Chinese ink
Size: 2.74 × 2.74 × 2.74 meters [9 × 9 × 9 feet]

In the summer of 2006, MAD placed a 2.74-meter (9-foot)
cube of ink-ice in the plaza of the China Millennium
Monument and left it to melt in the sun and wind for three
days. As the temperature warmed up, the solid entity gradually disappeared entirely. The only residue left behind
was a charcoal-black imprint on the ground. The abstract
symbols vanished, and a space for the imagination was
all that remained.

Superstar: A Mobile Chinatown
2008 / Venice, Italy / Neighborhood Concept

Superstar: A Mobile Chinatown was first exhibited in the Uneternal City section of the eleventh Venice Architecture Biennale. It is MAD's response to the redundant and increasingly out-of-date Chinatowns around the world. It is a mobile Chinatown, a home to 15,000 people that may land in any corner of the world, where it can lend new Chinese energy to the environment where it is located. It is a self-sustaining community that grows its own food, requires no resources from the host city, and recycles all its waste. It is a living place, with authentic Chinese nature and health resorts, sports facilities, and reservoirs that provide safe drinking water. It even includes a digital cemetery to remember the deceased. Like the Olympics, it is a traveling party that can journey to a new host city every four years.

Feelings Are Facts
Olafur Eliasson and Ma Yansong
April 4–June 20, 2010 / Ullens Center for Contemporary
Art, Beijing, China / Installation
Curators: Jérôme Sans and Guo Xiaoyan

Olafur Eliasson and Ma Yansong challenge our everyday
patterns of spatial orientation. Vision functions as our
primary, default sense for navigation, but this expansive
installation induces initial insecurity in its visitors by
radically reducing visibility, thereby suggesting the need
to invent new models for perception.